THE GREAT
Disneyland
SCAVENGER HUNT

THE GREAT
Disneyland
SCAVENGER HUNT

*A Detailed Path throughout the Disneyland &
Disney's California Adventure Parks*

Catherine F. Olen

New York

THE GREAT Disneyland SCAVENGER HUNT
A Detailed Path throughout the Disneyland &
Disney's California Adventure Parks
© 2016 Catherine F. Olen.

Published in New York, New York, by Morgan James Publishing. Morgan James and The Entrepreneurial Publisher are trademarks of Morgan James, LLC. www.MorganJamesPublishing.com

The Morgan James Speakers Group can bring authors to your live event. For more information or to book an event visit The Morgan James Speakers Group at www.TheMorganJamesSpeakersGroup.com.

ISBN 978-1-63047-776-9 paperback
ISBN 978-1-63047-777-6 eBook
Library of Congress Control Number: 2015914403

Shelfie

A **free** eBook edition is available
with the purchase of this print book.

CLEARLY PRINT YOUR NAME ABOVE IN UPPER CASE

Instructions to claim your free eBook edition:
1. Download the Shelfie app for Android or iOS
2. Write your name in **UPPER CASE** above
3. Use the Shelfie app to submit a photo
4. Download your eBook to any device

Cover Design by:
Rachel Lopez
www.r2cdesign.com

Interior Design by:
Bonnie Bushman
bonnie@caboodlegraphics.com

In an effort to support local communities and raise awareness and funds, Morgan James Publishing donates a percentage of all book sales for the life of each book to Habitat for Humanity Peninsula and Greater Williamsburg

Get involved today, visit
www.MorganJamesBuilds.com

Peninsula and
Greater Williamsburg
Building Partner

Dedication

I cannot thank my beautiful daughter, Brooke, enough for all her love and support throughout this process. You are the light of my life my lamb.

To Jeff for your unending belief in me when I could not see the light at the end of the tunnel

To Tom for your support of my dreams

To Lynne Dunn for being my twin in love of everything Disney

To John for being one of God's angels here on earth

Lastly, my thanks to Walt Disney for the vision that created Disneyland and all of the cast members who have made this adventure a magical experience.

Table of Contents

Disney's California Adventure

Introduction

Disneyland: just the sound of the name on your lips conjures visions of Mickey Mouse and Snow White, the Sleeping Beauty castle towering against the clear blue sky of Southern California, the thrilling experiences of Space Mountain, or the magical fireworks that light up the night sky.

My love affair with all things created by visionary Walt Disney began as a small child with our family's yearly pilgrimages to the Magic Kingdom. Memories of seeing the snow-capped peak of the Matterhorn as we exited the freeway and pulling into the vast parking lot with sections named after all of the beloved characters I had watched on the movie screen.

Seeing the front gates would foster giddy anticipation of the treasures just beyond the tunnels. The sights, smells and music of Main Street would be a blur as we rushed past the shops, knowing the delights waiting within the various lands.

As children we would rush up the draw bridge of Sleeping Beauty Castle hearing the strains of "Once Upon a Dream" growing louder as we emerged from the gates into the charming world of Fantasyland. My parents would purchase books of ride coupons, the A coupons going unused as we tried in vain to decide which attraction to use the precious E Coupons on. We would stand impatiently in line after line just to be transported to the world of Alice in Wonderland, Pinocchio and Pirates of the Caribbean.

As an adult, I found that the world of Disneyland slowed down and I could stroll through the various wonders of the theme park seeing for the first time with amazement the details that Walt Disney had so lovingly provided for the guests to experience. I could now take my time and stop rushing, experiencing each new delight while watching the thousands of guests breeze past the same things I had missed for so many years.

I invite you to use the pages within this book to see the Disneyland theme parks through new eyes. Whether this is your first visit or five hundredth, I challenge you to finish this book and not find something new to enjoy within the borders of the Disneyland resort.

This book is dedicated to the vision of Walt Disney.

Disneyland resort, built by creative thinker Walt Disney, from ground breaking to completion took one year. Disney took on the singular task of overseeing the entire construction of the theme park, ensuring no detail would be left out. He painstakingly spent the year creating an experience for the guests that would come through the gate for decades to come.

While Disneyland will never be complete, Walt Disney's spirit and dream remain a constant part of the charm Disneyland holds in the hearts of all who enter her gates.

How to use this book:

Your Disney trivia is broken down into three categories

- One star – Easier questions – Good for families with small children or first time guests
- Two star– Challenging questions – For returning guests and those with more time
- Three star– Expert questions – For those looking for a real challenge or Disney park experts

All of the questions found in this book have been verified by several Disney enthusiasts but I am aware that the décor of Disneyland changes regularly. If there are changes, you can visit www.MouseHangover.com for current updates. If you have come across a change prior to me, please email me so the changes can be noted.

I hope you find your way through the Disneyland resort with new eyes and enjoy your hunt for the loving details Walt Disney wanted his guests to experience.

Note: All content is subject to change without notice. Ride closures, construction, or overlays for the Halloween and

Christmas holidays may alter the content temporarily due to park-wide decorations.

Trademarks:

This book Disney copy-righted characters, registered trademarks, marks, and registered marks of The Walt Disney Company and Disney Enterprises Inc.

All references to these properties, and The Twilight Zone®, a registered trademark of CBS, Inc., are made solely for editorial purposes. Neither the author nor the publisher make any commercial claim to their use, and neither is affiliated with The Walt Disney Company or CBS in any way.

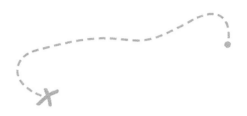

Esplanade

As you enter the front gates of Disneyland, the esplanade only hints at the wonders awaiting you beyond the tunnels. Stop for a moment to begin your memories by getting your picture in front of the Mickey Mouse flower display.

Having difficulty finding something on your scavenger hunt? Click the QR code or link at the bottom of the chapter to help you on your way.

1.   ★ Even before you enter the gates of the Magic Kingdom, the turnstiles stretch out before you. How many entrance and exit gates are there?

a. 16   c. 32

b. 20   d. 36

2. ★ As you look up at the Disneyland Railroad sign, what is the population of Disneyland?

a. 1 million   c. 600 million

b. 250 million   d. 650 million

3. ★ As you look up at the Disneyland Railroad sign, what is the elevation of Disneyland?

a. 138 feet   c. 318 feet

b. 158 feet   d. Sea level

4. ★ As you enter the tunnel to Main Street on either the right or left side, what is the tenth word in the dedication on the bronze plaque above your head?

a. Yesterday   c. World

b. Fantasy   d. Tomorrow

Did you know?

Disneyland has its own postal code, 92802. You can mail your post cards from Disneyland resort by dropping them into any of the mail-boxes throughout the theme park.

Looking for hints on your way? Click here to find what you seek.

Main Street U.S.A.

Main Street U.S.A. was fashioned after Walt Disney's beloved Marceline, Missouri at the turn of the century. Take a stroll back in time as you discover the wonders within this quaint street.

Having difficulty on your scavenger hunt? Click the link at the bottom of the chapter for hints to help you on your way.

1. ★★ As you enter through the tunnel on your left and arrive on Main Street U.S.A., you will arrive at City Hall. In front of the building there is a sign for lost parents; what famous Disney couple is featured on this sign?

    a.   Mr. and Mrs. Darling

    b.   Mr. and Mrs. Banks

    c.   Belle and Beast

    d.   Rapunzel and Flynn Rider

2.   ★ According to the window outside City Hall, what year was the "Price is Right" land company founded?

    a.   1965   c.   1971

    b.   1955   d.   1901

3.   ★ Within City Hall, you will find a book shelf. Which author appears on the book "Lillybelle"?

    a.   M. Isner   c.   M. Mouse

    b.   L.E. Disney   d.   W.E. Disney

Did you know?

You can get a birthday phone call from your Disney friends inside City Hall! Just ask one of the cast members. And remember to get a birthday button to celebrate your special day.

Disneyland Fire Station

4.   ★ Which number is displayed on the outside of the fire station?

    a.   1313   c.   105

    b.   33   d.   501

5.   ★ Within the fire station, which of these is *not* one of the departments shown on the injury roster?

    a.   722   c.   803

    b.   612   d.   912

6.   ★ Within the fire station, there is a clock on the wall. What time does the clock show?

a. 2:31   c. 5:02
b. 3:21   d. 9:32

7.   ★ What time span is covered by the fire logs on the shelf inside the fire station?

a. 1955 - 1971   c. 1984 - 1989
b. 1894 - 1899   d. 1901 - 1966

8.   ★★ What name is engraved on the wrench next to the Valiant Hose #2 sign?

a. Lillian   c. Greenberg
b. Disney   d. Valiant

9.   ★ What are the two names on the horse stalls within the fire station?

a. Jess and Bess   c. Mickey and Minnie
b. Walt and Lillian   d. Wess and Tess

Did you know?

Walt Disney built an apartment for himself above the fire station during the construction of Disneyland. He stayed on the property to oversee the construction and the light in the window would be lit when the Disney family was in residence. Look up at the window; you can see the light as a permanent memorial to Walt Disney.

Main Street Train Station

10.   ★ According to the brass plaque, what scale was the original Lilly Belle train Walt Disney later used as the model for the full size C.K. Holliday?

a. 1/2   c. 1/4th
b. 1/16th   d. 1/8th

11. ★ What number is displayed on the side of the Lilly Belle model within the glass case in the train station?

    a. 173   c. 371
    b. 137   d. 731

12. ★★ Which of these is *not* one of the names of the listed Disneyland train engine?

    a. E.P. Ripley   c. Ward Kimball
    b. Fred Gurley   d. Bill Justice

13. ★★ As you look at the right shadow box on the wall, what number is displayed on the yellow train ticket displayed inside the shadow box?

    a. 005564   c. 004565
    b. 006545   d. 005646

14. ★★ According to the train tickets on display, which is *not* one of the Frontierland attractions listed?

    a. Steamboat
    b. Cattle Train
    c. Big Thunder Mountain
    d. Frontierland Stockade

15. ★★ What U.S. City manufactured the nickelodeon on display within the train station?

    a. Los Angeles   c. New York
    b. Chicago   d. Marceline

16. ★ According to the "Walt and Steam Locomotive" plaque, what was the name of the iron works Walt Disney created?

    a. Ripley   c. Broggie
    b. Kimball   d. Gurley

17.   ★ What is the name on the scale featured in the Main Street train station?

    a.   Disney   c.   Ripley

    b.   Kimball   d.   Watling

18.   ★★ As you look in the ticket window outside the Main Street station, there is a scale model train, "The Philadelphia," on display. What is the date on the model?

    a.   1955   c.   1871

    b.   1901   d.   1971

19.   ★★ As you look in the ticket window outside the Main Street station, which of these is *not* one of the numbers written on the chalk board?

    a.   2   c.   5

    b.   4   d.   6

Did you know?

You can make a request with the conductor to ride in the "Lilly Belle," the caboose decorated by Lillian Disney and used for dignitaries.

You can also request a "Tinder Ride", riding in the front with the engineers. These options do not allow for passengers to exit at any stops except for Main Street station.

Disneyana

Did you know?

The Disneyana shop was originally the Main Street bank and was converted to a store after ATMs made money more available to guests. Bank of America worked seven days a week offering Disneyland guests access to cash and Disney Dollars.

20. ★ As you stand outside the "Disneyana" store on Main Street, there is a mural on the wall on the right side of the building. What time is on the clock displayed?

a. 2:55   c. 1:55

b. 3:55   d. 2:05

21. ★ Within the "Disneyana" store, which previously held the Disneyland bank, there is a vault; what is the name of the safe company?

a. Disney Safe Co.   c. Carter Safe Co.

b. Mosler Safe Co.   d. Langdon Safe Co.

Main Street Opera House

22. ★ Which of these is *not* one of the items on display from Griffith Park, where Walt Disney first dreamed Disneyland?

a. Park bench

b. Merry-go-round horse

c. Drinking fountain

d. Peanut cart

23. ★★ According to the plaque below the photograph of Walt Disney, which is the seventeenth word in his opening day speech?

a. Memories   c. Future

b. Fond   d. Savor

24. ★ Within the opera house, there is a map of the original Disneyland Park; which animated character sits between "e" and "y" in Disneyland at the bottom of the map?

a. Genie   c. Aladdin

b. Crocodile   d. Jasmine

25.   ★ According to the legend on the original Disneyland map, what is the scale size?

a.   1:1000   c.   1:100

b.   1:10   d.   1:1

26.   ★ Displayed on the wall is a copy of the "The Disneyland News" from July 1955. According to the headline, how many people attended the gala park opening?

a.   50,000   c.   100,000

b.   10,000   d.   1,000,000

27.   ★★ Read "The Disneyland News" displayed on the wall next to the large map. According to the article on subscriptions, how much was the monthly edition of "The Disneyland News"?

a. $1.50   c. $1.70

b. $2.25   d. $1.20

28.   ★★ As you watch the introduction video for the opera house, what animated character cohosts with actor Steve Martin?

a.   Mickey Mouse   c.   Goofy

b.   Donald Duck   d.   Minnie Mouse

29.   ★★ According to the "Creating Great Moments" plaque, what year did the Great moments with Mr. Lincoln attraction appear at the Main Street Opera House?

a.   1955   c.   1971

b.   1965   d.   1995

30.   ★ On display are various statues depicting the various spirits of America; which character is depicted in the Spirit of Individualism?

a.   Sea Captain   c.   Cowboy

b.   Mother   d.   Aviator

31.   ★ What great historical monument is on display within the Main Street Opera House?

a.   The White House

b.   The Lincoln Memorial

c.   The Washington Memorial

d.   The Capitol Building

32.   ★★ According to the "Lincoln's Gettysburg Speech" plaque, finish the sentence: "It is for us, the living rather to be dedicated here to the _____"

a.   Unfinished Work   c.   A New Nation

b.   Birth of Freedom   d.   Honored Soldiers

33.   ★ What year was the Gettysburg Address speech given by Abraham Lincoln according to the "Lincoln's Gettysburg Speech" plaque?

a.   1763   c.   1683

b.   1963   d.   1863

34.   ★ To the right of the entrance to the theater you will find a photograph of Walt Disney as a young boy with his childhood friend; what is the name of Walt's friend according to the brass plaque?

a.   Walt Pfieffer   c.   Mickey Pfieffer

b.   Roy Pfieffer   d.   Ub Iwerks

35.   ★★ At the exit to "Great Moments with Mr. Lincoln", what famous comedic actress adorns the wall on the right of the exit doors?

a.   Lucille Ball   c.   Gilda Radner

b.   Madeline Kahn   d.   Betty White

36. ★ At the exit to "Great Moments with Mr. Lincoln", which of these is *not* one of the spirits shown?

a. Perseverance   c. Tolerance

b. Inspiration   d. Determination

37. ★ Upon exiting the Opera House building, you will find a mailbox. What is the year printed on the side of this mailbox?

a. 1955   c. 1971

b. 1948   d. 1999

Main Street Magic

Did you know?

As you peer into the front windows of the Main Street Magic Shop, you will find authentic magic props owned and used by the famous Harry Houdini. These items are on permanent display for the guests to peruse.

38. ★★ As you make your way down Main Street U.S.A., enter the Magic Shop on your right. What famous comedian has a signed photograph on the wall behind the counter?

a. Bob Hope   c. Jim Belushi

b. Milton Berle   d. Steve Martin

39. ★ On the wall of the Magic Shop you will find an antique phone. Which famous magician is credited with supplying the recording you hear when you lift the receiver?

    a.   Harry Houdini   c.   Chris Angel

    b.   David Copperfield   d.   Penn & Teller

Did you know?

You can ask the magicians within the Magic Shop to perform for you! Ask one of these talented performers to demonstrate the levitating card trick.

Emporium

40. ★★★ As you cross the street to the Emporium, how many light bulbs make up the word "Emporium"?

    a.   89   c.   98

    b.   100   d.   198

41. ★★ As you enter the Emporium, look at the large shadow boxes above the room. Which of these scenes is *not* depicted in one of the boxes?

    a.   Millinery   c.   Tailor

    b.   Barbershop   d.   Dentist

Main Street Cinema

42. ★ As you continue down Main Street, The Main Street Cinema is on your right. What is the name of the ticket seller in the booth?

    a.   Milly   c.   Sally

    b.   Tilly   d.   Lillian

43. ★ According to the movie posters outside the cinema, what is the name of the dog that's been dog-napped?

    a.   Pluto   c.   Fifi

    b.   Didi   d.   Goofy

44. ★ What is printed on the tickets displayed in the ticket booth?
    a. Identification Check
    b. Admit One
    c. Premier
    d. Main Street Cinema

Did you know?

The classic cartoons exhibited within the Main Street Cinema have been playing continually for guests since Disneyland's opening in 1955.

It is commonly mistaken that *Steamboat Willie* was the first Disney cartoon created. In actuality, *Plane Crazy*, a silent film, was the first created though it could not find distribution. *Steamboat Willie* was released as the first sound animated short and *Plane Crazy* was released after with the addition of sound.

---

45. ★★ As you stroll down Main Street U.S.A., look at the windows high above your head; what is the established date of the Elias Disney Contractor window?
    a. 1985   c. 1901
    b. 1895   d. 1955

46. ★ Next door to the Main Street Cinema, you will find the Disneyland Casting Agency door. Finish the sentence, "It takes _____ to make the dream a reality."
    a. Magic   c. People
    b. Fantasy   d. Money

47. ★ On the "Casting Agency" newspaper on the wall next to the door, what is the requirement for the ragtime piano player?

    a. Classical training   c. Own a piano

    b. No moustache   d. No drinking

48.   ★ On the "Casting Agency" newspaper on the wall next to the door, what is optional for the Pirate Crew casting?

    a.   Eye patch   c.   Sword Play

    b.   Parrot   d.   Gun

49.   ★ On the "Casting Agency" newspaper on the wall next to the door, which railroad should the train conductors contact?

    a.   Santa Fe   c.   W.E Disney

    b.   Pacific   d.   Carolwood

Crystal Arcade

50.   ★ On the left side of Main Street U.S.A. you will see the Crystal Arcade. What is the number on the building?

    a.   701   c.   107

    b.   501   d.   105

51.   ★ As you enter the Crystal Arcade, walk to the back of the store and you will see two etched glass signs. According to the sign on your right, what year was Emporium established?

    a.   1955   c.   1971

    b.   1855   d.   1901

52.   ★★ As you enter the toy section on your right, you will see classic characters lining the walls above you; what playground attraction do Robin Hood and Maid Marian sit upon?

    a.   Swings   c.   Teeter Totter

    b.   Carousel   d.   Slide

53. ★★ As you continue looking to your right at the dioramas, which villain is standing beside the smiling full moon?

   a. Cruella De Vil   c. Scar

   b. Jafar   d. Captain Hook

Penny Arcade

54. ★ As you continue your tour of Main Street U.S.A., what is the name of the gypsy fortune teller that sits at the entrance to Penny Arcade?

   a. Esmeralda   c. Madam Leota

   b. Emerald   d. Minnie

55. ★ According to the penny flickers at the entrance to Penny Arcade, what is the name of the actor starring in *The Big Beauty Buster*?

   a. Charlie Chaplin   c. Buster Keaton

   b. Bull Montana   d. Stan Laurel

56. ★★ According to the Kiss-O-Meter in Crystal Arcade, which of these is the maximum rating?

   a. Dynamite   c. Passionate

   b. Devastating   d. Thrilling

57. ★★ Which one of the penny flickers within Penny Arcade stars the great Charlie Chaplin?

   a. *Forbidden Sweets*

   b. *Monkey Business*

   c. *The Adventures of Charlie Chaplin*

   d. *Just Desserts*

58.　★★ At the back wall of Penny Arcade stands a nickelodeon; what is the name of the company that manufactured this musical wonder?

a. Wurlitzer
b. Disney & Disney
c. Kurzweiler
d. M. Welte & Sohne

Did you know?

This antique nickelodeon plays classic Disney songs every seven minutes. Stay for a while to hear your favorite songs and marvel at the engineering wonder before you.

Did you know?

As you exit the Candy Palace, stop and watch the candy makers create your favorite sweet treats in the window. Take a moment to smell the scent of vanilla in the air and look at the vents below the window. Disney pumps the scent into the air to help guests get in the candy mood.

59.　★ As you cross Main Street U.S.A., you will see an alley next to Market House. As you enter look at the windows above you to the right; what is the tag line for the Detective Agency?

a. "We Always Get Our Man"
b. "We Never Sleep"
c. "We Never Sleep in Any Time Zone"
d. "Private Eye"

60.　★★★ As you continue to down the alley, listen to the lesson taught on the second floor to your left. What is she teaching?

a. Singing
b. Piano
c. Flute
d. Drums

Did you know?

The wall to the right of the locker area has several different styles of bricks. Walt Disney used this wall during construction of Disneyland to select the brick styles for the various areas of Disneyland, and the wall was left in its original state after the park opened.

---

61.   ★★ As you look across the alley, what is the Dental School licensed to use according to the sign on the door?

    a.   Laughing Gas   c.   Pixie Dust

    b.   Dental Floss   d.   Pliers

Disney Clothiers

62.   ★★ As you enter Disney Clothiers, continue to the room selling baby clothing. Look around you at the shelves around the perimeter of the room. Which famous Disney characters stand on the miniature toy box?

    a.   Lady and the Tramp

    b.   Mickey and Minnie

    c.   Peter Pan and Tinker Bell

    d.   Donald and Daisy

63.   ★ Within the baby section of Disney Clothiers, which figure can you find standing sentinel in this room?

    a.   Suit of Armor   c.   Policeman

    b.   Cigar Store Indian   d.   Wooden Solider

64.   ★ As you enter the Men's section of Disney Clothiers, look at the frames on the wall above the cash register. You will find a frame with twelve pennants. Which school is represented in the lower right corner?

a.   Missouri   c.   Georgia

b.   Purdue   d.   Michigan

65.   ★★★ As you exit this store back to Main Street, you will see a porch to your right with chairs for you to rest on during your visit. What store occupied this space when Disneyland opened in 1955?

a.   Carnation Café   c.   Magic Shop

b.   China Closet   d.   Wizard of Bras

66.   ★★★ Continue down Main Street U.S.A., turn the corner at Main Street Photo Supply, and on your right you will find the Child Care center. Within the lobby, you will find an infant's portrait. Who is the infant in this portrait?

a.   Walt Disney   c.   Elias Disney

b.   Roy Disney   d.   Lillian Disney

Did you know?

As you come back to Main Street U.S.A., stop at Coca Cola corner and stand under the awning at the corner. Look up at the lights and you will notice one light is dual colored. When installing the lights, they installed an odd number of bulbs so the installer created a bulb with both red and white to keep the count even.

Looking for hints on your way? Click here to find what you seek.

Hub

The hub of Disneyland is a wheel-spoke design to give guests easy access to all of the lands. This area has been host to some of the greatest Disney legends during the various celebrations from the beginnings of Disneyland.

Having difficulty on your scavenger hunt? Click the link at the bottom of the chapter for hints to help you on your way.

1.　　★ As you enter the hub, look to the right side at the popcorn cart. What figure is cranking the popcorn inside?

a.　Mickey Mouse　　　c.　Clown

b.　Donald Duck　　　　d.　Goofy

2.   ★ At the center of the hub of Disneyland you will find the statue of Walt Disney and Mickey Mouse. What is the name of this statue?

    a.   Friends   c.   Partners

    b.   Started by a Mouse   d.   Walt and Mickey

3.   ★ As you read the plaque at the base of this statue, which of these is *not* one of the tributes listed?

    a.   Dreams   c.   Creativity

    b.   Fantasy   d.   Vision

4.   ★★ As you stand at the hub, look around you at the characters. Which of these is *not* one of the characters included in the hub statuary?

    a.   Pinocchio   c.   Dumbo

    b.   White Rabbit   d.   Tinker Bell

Looking for hints on your way? Click here to find what you seek.

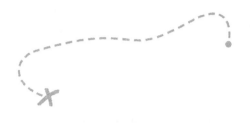

Fantasyland

Cross over the draw bridge and relive your favorite animated classic. Become a prince or princess, go on a wild ride, or fly above the rooftops of London. Within Fantasyland your fondest childhood dreams become reality when you fly on Dumbo and spin the teacups on your own mad tea party.

Having difficulty on your scavenger hunt? Click the link at the bottom of the chapter for hints to help you on your way.

Sleeping Beauty Castle

1.   ★ As you walk toward Sleeping Beauty Castle, look down at the ground in front of the castle. What famous quote is displayed around the compass on the ground?
   a. "When you wish upon a star, your dreams come true"
   b. "It all started with a mouse"
   c. "A dream is a wish your heart makes"
   d. Someday my prince will come"

2.   ★ In front of the castle you will find a bronze plaque for the "Disneyland Time Castle." What is the date this was placed in the ground?
   a. July 17. 1955   c. July 17, 1995
   b. July 17 1895   d. July 17, 2005

3.   ★ In what year will the "Disneyland Time Castle" be opened?
   a. 2015   c. 2035
   b. 2025   d. 2055

Did you know?

The drawbridge of Sleeping Beauty Castle is a working drawbridge. It was opened only twice, once on opening day July 27, 1955, and once again in 1983 for the dedication of the new Fantasyland.

---

4.   ★★★ As you walk up the drawbridge of Sleeping Beauty castle, look up at the apex of the archway. You will see a crest with three lions. What does this symbolize?
   a. Disneyland Logo
   b. Disney family crest

c. Mickey Mouse crest

d. The key to Disneyland

5. ★ As you look at the front of Sleeping Beauty castle, you will notice the water spouts adorning the front of the castle. What woodland creature is the figure of these water spouts?

a. Mice   c. Fish

b. Birds   d. Squirrels

6. ★ As you cross the drawbridge of Sleeping Beauty Castle into Fantasyland, look at the wall to your right of the prince kissing Sleeping Beauty. Finish the quote found below: "When true love's kiss the spell shall _____."

a. Wake   c. Take

b. Break   d. Make

7. ★ On the wall to your left you will see a mosaic of the prince fighting the dragon Maleficent. Finish the quote found below: "Oh sword of truth fly swift and _____."

a. Pure   c. Endure

b. Cure   d. Sure

Did you know?

If you look at the ground just inside the castle gate in Fantasyland, you will find a gold spike in the ground. This has been mistakenly thought to be the center of Disneyland on opening day. In actuality, this is a survey marker, one of many you will find around the Disneyland resort. The center of Disneyland is within the hub where the Partners statue is located.

8.   ★ As you enter Fantasyland, walk to your right and you will find the entrance to the Sleeping Beauty walk through. As you enter, you will see the first story book. How many trumpeters appear on the page?

a.   3   c.   5
b.   4   d.   1

9.   ★★ As you continue up the stairs of this attraction, you will come to the first window. What is being burned as the king and queen watch?

a.   Briar thorns   c.   Spinning Wheels
b.   Crowns   d.   Fire wood

10.   ★ As you continue through the castle, according to the storybook, what object lured Princess Aurora to the tower on her sixteenth birthday?

a.   Spinning wheel   c.   Good fairies
b.   Green light   d.   Maleficent's raven

11.   ★ As you see Princess Aurora sleeping on the castle floor, what color dress is she wearing?

a.   White   c.   Blue
b.   Pink   d.   Rose

12.   ★ According to the next story book, how long would the kingdom stay asleep?

a.   100 years
b.   10 days
c.   Eternity
d.   Till the princess awakes

> **Did you know?**
> As you reach the top of Sleeping Beauty Castle, there is a door to your right with a knob. If you pull on the knob, the door shakes and voices laugh maniacally. And if you watch the door to the right, you will see the spear of Maleficent's goon guarding the other side of this door.

13. ★ According to the next storybook, what did Maleficent summon to stop the prince from reaching the princess?

   a. Thorns   c. Ghosts
   b. Flames   d. Demons

14. ★ As you continue through the attraction to the window where the prince fights Maleficent, what form does she turn into?

   a. Dragon   c. Thorns
   b. Bat   d. Warrior

15. ★ As you begin down the stairs after the fight scene, pause for a moment. What character shadow appears on the wall in front of you?

   a. Sleeping Beauty c. The Prince
   b. Maleficent   d. The Fairies

16. ★ As you exit this attraction, you will see one final storybook. What are the words on the page?

   a. They Lived Happily Ever After
   b. The End
   c. True Love's Kiss
   d. Sleeping Beauty

17. ★★ As you walk towards the Bibbidi Bobbidi Boutique, look up at the eves in front of the shop. Which of these characters is *not* seen on the posts?

a. Captain Hook   c. Mr. Smee

b. Crocodile   d. Peter Pan

18. ★★ High above Snow White's Scary Adventure, you will find a castle window. What figure appears when the curtain is drawn back?

a. Snow White   c. The Evil Queen

b. Prince Charming   d. Dopey

Snow White's Scary Adventure

19. ★★ As you enter the queue for Snow White's Scary Adventure, you will see a gold book atop a pedestal. What is the first word that appears at the top of the right page?

a. Apple   c. Evil

b. Danger   d. Beware

20. ★ As you continue in the queue, you will see the dungeon to your left. What does the book say will happen if you taste the poison apple?

    a. Sleeping Death

    b. Sick to your Stomach

    c. Get lost in the woods

    d. Enter the Dungeon

21. ★★ As you enter the ride vehicle and your journey begins, what woodland creature holds the "Beware" sign?

    a. Squirrel   c. Bluebird

    b. Owl   d. Chipmunk

22. ★★★ As you enter the dwarves' house, what color is the sock the chipmunk is holding?

    a. Blue and green   c. White

    b. Green and yellow   d. Red and white

23. ★★★ You will see the dwarves playing their instruments for Snow White. Which dwarf is playing the organ?

    a. Happy   c. Grumpy

    b. Dopey   d. Sneezy

24. ★★ As you see the sign for the diamond mine, what structure do you see in the distance?

    a. The Evil Queen's Castle

    b. The Prince's Castle

    c. The Dwarves' House

    d. The Town

25. ★★ What two creatures sit atop the tree as you enter the Evil Queen's castle?

    a. Rats   c. Ravens

    b. Bats   d. Vultures

26. ★★ What creature adorns the back of the Evil Queen's throne?

    a. Lion
    b. Peacock
    c. Horse
    d. Bat

27. ★ As the Evil Queen appears from under the bridge, what color are the apples in her basket?

    a. Red
    b. Brown
    c. Yellow
    d. Green

28. ★★★ In the scary forest scene, what animal do the fallen logs become?

    a. Snakes
    b. Crocodiles
    c. Fish
    d. Tigers

29. ★★★ When you see the dwarves chasing the Evil Queen up the cliff, which dwarf is last, holding the candle?

    a. Grumpy
    b. Dopey
    c. Happy
    d. Bashful

30. ★★★ How many times during Snow White's Scary Adventure do you encounter the Evil Queen?

    a. 5
    b. 4
    c. 3
    d. 6

31. ★ As you come to the exit of Snow White's Scary Adventure, what item sits atop the cast member console?

    a. Raven
    b. Candle
    c. Skull
    d. Crown

32. ★★★ As you exit the ride vehicle, look at the mural on the wall. Which of the seven dwarves is winking at you?

    a. Doc
    b. Dopey
    c. Happy
    d. Grumpy

Peter Pan's Flight

33. ★★ As you are standing in the queue for Peter Pan's Flight, you will see a mural behind the loading area. Which famous landmark do you see in the skyline?

   a. Big Ben
   c. The Pyramids
   b. Eiffel Tower
   d. The Acropolis

34. ★★ As you enter the pirate ship, look closely at the area around you. Where are you as you enter the ride?

   a. London Bridge
   c. Lost Boys Hideout
   b. On the street
   d. The rooftops

35. ★★★ When you enter the Darling children's bedroom, what do the blocks scattered on the floor spell out?

   a. Wendy
   c. P Pan
   b. John
   d. Michael

36. ★★ As you fly over London, what can you see beyond the clouds?

   a. One star
   c. Tinker Bell
   b. Two stars
   d. Nana

37. ★ As you fly over the island of Neverland, what do you see over the lagoon?

   a. Clouds
   c. A ship
   b. A rainbow
   d. Nana the dog

38. ★★★ As you approach skull rock, which character is tied up in the water?

   a. Peter Pan
   c. Tiger Lily
   b. Wendy
   d. Mr. Smee

39. ★★ As you fly over the pirate ship, you will see the Indian village. How many Indians are seen sitting by the fire?

a. 2   c. 5
b. 3   d. 4

40.   ★ As we see Captain Hook for the last time, what word
       do you hear him yell out?
       a. "Smee!"   c. "Tink!"
       b. "Pan!"   d. "No!"

- -

Did you know?

As your pirate ship approaches the exit queue, look to your right
just before you make the turn. There is a tree with a round hinged
cover disguising the entrance to the Lost Boys Hide-out.

- -

41.   ★ As you exit your pirate ship, look to your left. How
       many Mermaids are preening on the rocks?
       a. 4   c. 3
       b. 5   d. 1

Pinocchio's Daring Journey

42.   ★ As you approach Pinocchio's Daring Journey, what
       barnyard animal is featured with Pinocchio atop the
       entrance?
       a. Horse   c. Chicken
       b. Cow   d. Sheep

43.   ★★ As you enter the queue, look at the mural beyond
       the loading queue. Which of these is *not* featured on the
       signpost?
       a. School   c. Stromboli's Theater
       b. Gepetto's house   d. Pleasure Island

44. ★★ Look at the mural beyond the loading queue. What is The Coachman holding in his hands?

    a. A whip   c. A marionette
    b. Dollar bills   d. Bags of gold

45. ★★ As you enter your ride vehicle, look at the carving on the side. Which two characters adorn the side of your car?

    a. Gepetto and Pinocchio
    b. Pinocchio and Lampwick
    c. Cleo and Figaro
    d. Blue Fairy and Cleo

46. ★★ As you enter the theater, which marionette stands to Pinocchio's right?

    a. Can-can girl   c. Toy soldier
    b. Dutch girl   d. Ballerina

47. ★★★ When you see Stromboli standing at the top of the stairs, what does he hold in his left hand?

    a. A rope   c. A lock
    b. A marionette   d. A cage

48. ★★ As you escape from Stromboli and head toward the village, what color is the umbrella holding Jiminy Cricket?

    a. Blue   c. Black
    b. Green   d. Red

49. ★ As you exit the candy store on Pleasure Island, what does the stand outside sell?

    a. Churro's   c. Soda Pop
    b. Popcorn   d. Lollypops

50. ★★ As you pass through Pleasure Island, What carnival game does Gideon the cat play with Honest John?

    a.   Ring Toss   c.   Go Fish

    b.   Knock the Cans   d.   Ring the Bell

51.   ★★★ As you continue in Pleasure Island, what building sits at the end of Tobacco Road?

    a.   The Rough House   c.   Candy store

    b.   The pool hall   d.   School

52.   ★★ As you enter the Pool Hall, what sits high atop the rafters?

    a.   Cigars   c.   Money bags

    b.   Pool cues   d.   Moonshine jugs

53.   ★★ As you exit the pool hall, what famous work of art do you see destroyed?

    a.   Venus De Milo

    b.   The Thinker

    c.   The Mona Lisa

    d.   Madonna on the Rocks

54.   ★★ What sign appears on the large crate you almost get caught in?

    a. To The Village   c. Handle with Care

    b. To The Salt Mines   d. Delivery to Gepetto

55.   ★★ What do you hear Jiminy Cricket yell out as Monstro the whale appears?

    a.   "Pinocchio!"   c.   "Watch Out!"

    b.   "This Way!"   d.   "You're Safe!"

56.   ★ As you enter Geppetto's Toy shop, what is Figaro the cat doing while Pinocchio becomes a real boy?

    a.   Lying in bed

    b.   Dancing with Cleo

c. Sitting on the window sill

d. Eating his dinner

57. ★ As you come to the exit queue, what character is featured on the mural to the left?

a. Pinocchio   c. Jiminy Cricket

b. The Blue Fairy   d. Gepetto

King Arthur's Carousel

58. ★ As you walk through Fantasyland, notice the Sword in the Stone standing before King Arthur's Carousel. As you read the inscription, finish this line: "Whoso pulleth out this sword of this stone and anvil is _____ ruler born of England."

a. Rightwise   c. Crowned

b. Declared   d. Leftwise

59. ★★ As you watch the horses of King Arthur's Carousel, what color is the harness across the nose of the horse with the gold tooth?

a. Red   c. Orange

b. Yellow   d. Black

Did you know?

The lead horse on King Arthur's Carousel is Jingles. You will find her with gold leaf bells hanging from her saddle. She was dedicated to Julie Andrews in 2008 at a formal ceremony.

60. ★★★ As you look at Jingles, how many bells total are there on her harness and saddle?

a. 66   c. 58
b. 232   d. 72

Mr. Toad's Wild Ride

61. ★ As you look at Mr. Toad's house, how many chimneys do you see on the rooftop?

a. 8   c. 12
b. 6   d. 10

62. ★ As you look at the front of Mr. Toad's house, what are the words on the scroll of Toad's coat of arms?

a. Semper Disneyanus   c. Toadi Absurdus
b. Toadus Tiranus   d. Semper Absurda

63. ★ As you enter the front doors of the house, you will see a mural of Mr. Toad and friends. What does the sign at the bridge read?

a. Ratty's House   c. This Way
b. Toad's House   d. Nowhere Road

64. ★ As you look up at the rafters of Toad's house, what animals do you see along the ceiling?

a. Badgers   c. Rats
b. Toads   d. Ducks

Did you know?

As you continue in the queue for Mr. Toad's Wild Ride, you will pass a statue of Toad. You will notice that his hands are behind his back. When this statue was first installed, Mr. Toad was holding a monocle in his hand which was broken off shortly after. Many guests attempted to put various items between Mr. Toad's fingers so his hands were placed in this position to discourage guests from this practice.

65. ★★ During your wild ride, you will enter the library; how many books are there in Mole's hand?
    a. 3   c. 6
    b. 4   d. 10

66. ★★★ What is the name on the suit of armor that falls over as you drive by?
    a. Sir Clinksalot   c. Sir Mickey
    b. Sir Galahad   d. Sir Lancelot

67. ★★ As you enter the portrait hall, what activity is Toad doing in the first painting on your left?
    a. Bowling   c. Baking
    b. Boxing   d. Painting

68. ★★ As you enter the dining room, what is Toad's friend holding in his hand?
    a. Corn   c. Glass
    b. Fork   d. Chicken leg

69. ★★★ As you exit the house, what is the number on the policeman's uniform who tries to stop you?
    a. 13   c. 14
    b. 41   d. 243

70. ★★ As you continue your wild ride, how many sheep are in the cart atop the bridge you pass?
    a. 6   c. 10
    b. 4   d. 1

71. ★ As you enter Blinkey's Pub, what is the bartender holding in his hands?
    a. Wine bottles   c. Nothing
    b. Beer mugs   d. Cleaning rags

72. ★★ As you enter the courtroom, what does the barrister say to you?
    a. "Innocent!"
    b. "Dismissed"
    c. "Guilty! Thank you, that is all"
    d. "Take him away"

73. ★★★ As you reach the exit queue, what famous painting is Toad recreating?
    a. Pinkie
    b. Mona Lisa
    c. Starry Night
    d. Blue Boy

Casey Junior Circus Train

74. ★ Across Fantasyland is the Casey Junior Circus Train. As you enter the queue and enter the train, what is written on the pink cage?
    a. Circus Animals
    b. Casey Junior
    c. Monkeys
    d. Caboose

75. ★★ As Casey Junior comes around the track, what does the engine say as it climbs the hill?
    a. "I think I can!"
    b. "Casey Junior!"
    c. "I don't think I can."
    d. "I tried my best."

76. ★ How many train cars are there on the Casey Junior Circus Train?
    a. 3
    b. 6
    c. 8
    d. 10

Dumbo

77. ★ As you look at the Dumbo attraction, what animal sits high atop the hot air balloon?

    a. Mouse
    c. Stork
    b. Elephant
    d. Bear

78. ★★ What is the total number of Dumbo elephants on this attraction?

    a. 10
    c. 16
    b. 25
    d. 4

Did you know?

Toward the hedge behind the Dumbo attraction is an antique nickelodeon, take a moment the listen to the music.

Also in this area, you will notice a Dumbo vehicle inside in which you can pose for pictures.

---

79. ★ As you walk across Fantasyland, you will see the Mad Hatter hat shop. As you walk to the entrance, look up at the sign. Which character's name is embroidered on the mouse ears?

    a. Mad Hatter
    c. White Rabbit
    b. Alice
    d. Tweedle Dee

80. ★★★ As you enter the shop, look up at the rafters. How many carrots are painted on these rafters?

    a. 59
    c. 100
    b. 40
    d. 63

81.   ★ As you look at the mirror beyond the counter, which character from Alice in Wonderland appears as you gaze into the mirror?

    a. Caterpillar   c. Cheshire Cat

    b. Alice   d. Mad Hatter

82.   ★★ If you look at the window display of the tea party, what color is the cake in the center of the table?

    a. Pink   c. Green

    b. Blue   d. White

83.   ★ As you look at the picture with the yellow frame above the doorway, how many bunnies are featured in this family photo?

    a. 8   c. 10

    b. 9   d. 11

Storybook Land Canal Boats

Did you know?

The lighthouse that stands at the entrance to the Storybook Land Canal Boats is one of the last remaining ticket booths in Disneyland. Guest came to this location to purchase the coupons required for each attraction at Disneyland.

84.   ★★ As you approach the Storybook Land attraction you will notice Monstro the whale. How many teeth are in Monstro's mouth?

    a. 34   c. 54

    b. 24   d. 44

Did you know?

As you look at Monstro, watch carefully. Monstro winks his eye at you and he blows air and water from his blowhole.

85. ★ As you enter Storybook Land, which fairy tale is depicted first by your captain?

   a. Pinocchio
   b. The Three Little Pigs
   c. Aladdin
   d. Peter Pan

86. ★★ What building sits at the water's edge in the Alice in Wonderland village?

   a. Church
   b. Alice's house
   c. The Water Wheel
   d. Castle

87. ★★ What Disney character is seen as a golden statue in the center of London Park?

   a. Peter Pan
   b. Mickey Mouse
   c. Tinker Bell
   d. Wendy Darling

88. ★★ Listen carefully as you float beneath the rose-covered arches. What famous Disney love song is playing?

   a. Beauty and the Beast
   b. So this is Love
   c. A Whole New World
   d. Once Upon a Dream

89. ★★★ As you approach Snow White's section, what item do you see at the entrance to the dwarves' mine?

   a. Pickaxe
   b. Mine car
   c. Dynamite box
   d. Picnic lunch

90. ★ In Cinderella's village, what item sits halfway up the road to the castle?

    a. Glass slipper   c. Dog
    b. Mice   d. Pumpkin

91. ★ What color is the castle in the Cinderella village?

    a. White   c. Pink
    b. Gold   d. Green

92. ★ What is the patchwork quilt to your right made of?

    a. Desert plants   c. Miniature trees
    b. Fabric   d. Grass

93. ★ What famous Disney cartoon made this patchwork quilt to your left famous?

    a. *Lullaby Land*   c. *Steamboat Willie*
    b. *The Three Mills*   d. *Plane Crazy*

94. ★★ Who is the only person who knows the magical process to keep the plants in Storybook Land so small?

    a. Mickey Mouse   c. Tinker Bell
    b. Peter Pan   d. Genie

95. ★ Which castle is the last scene you see as you finish your Storybook Land cruise?

    a. Cinderella's castle   c. Jasmine's castle
    b. King Triton's castle   d. Elsa's castle

96. ★★ Which of these is *not* one of the fairy tales you experienced on The Storybook Land Canal Boats?

    a. Snow White
    b. Alice in Wonderland
    c. Frozen
    d. The Three Mills

Mad Tea Party

97. ★ What color is the tea cup sitting outside the Mad Hatter shop for photo opportunities?

    a. Blue   c. Lavender
    b. Green   d. Pink

98. ★ As you approach the queue for the Mad Tea Party, you will see a sign with the Mad Hatter pouring tea. How many cups is the Mad Hatter holding?

    a. 4   c. 3
    b. 5   d. 10

99. ★★ How many tea cups are there total on the Mad Tea Party attraction?

    a. 16   c. 20
    b. 18   d. 22

Alice in Wonderland

Did you know?

The enormous yellow mushroom that stands at the entrance to Alice in Wonderland is one of the last remaining ticket booths from the beginnings of Disneyland. Guests came to this location to purchase the coupons required for each attraction within Disneyland.

100. ★ As you gaze up at the large book atop the mushroom, what color is the letter *A* in Alice?

    a. Pink   c. Green
    b. Blue   d. Yellow

101. ★ On the left side of this attraction sit two birds on the rocks. What shape are the birds' heads?

    a. Shovel   c. Screwdriver

    b. Umbrella   d. Hammer

102. ★ Which character from *Alice in Wonderland* adorns the left side of the attraction perched in the rocks?

    a. Alice   c. Cheshire Cat

    b. Caterpillar   d. White Rabbit

103. ★★ As you enter the queue, watch the caterpillar ride vehicles. Which of these is *not* one of the colors you see?

    a. Pink   c. Blue

    b. White   d. Green

104. ★ What does the doorknob say to you as you fall down the rabbit hole?

    a. "Looking for the White Rabbit?"

    b. "I'm Locked."

    c. "You're going the wrong way!"

    d. "Looking for the Queen?"

105. ★ What color are the flags atop the hats of Tweedle Dee and Tweedle Dum?

    a. Red   c. Blue

    b. Yellow   d. White

106. ★★ As you enter the garden, what song are the flowers singing to you?

    a. "The Unbirthday Song"

    b. "Very Good Advice"

    c. "Golden Afternoon"

    d. "Shy Little Violets"

107. ★★ You will find the caterpillar sitting in the garden. How many arms and legs does the Caterpillar have in total?

    a. 4   c. 10

    b. 8   d. 12

108. ★★ What do the flowers call you when the Caterpillar asks, "Who are you?"

    a. Flowers   c. Weeds

    b. Humans   d. Dandelions

109. ★★★ As you enter Tulgey Woods, which of these is *not* one of the signs you read?

    a. This Way   c. Yonder

    b. Beyond   d. Down

110. ★★ What object does the owl in Tulgey Woods emulate?

    a. Accordion   c. Horn

    b. Pencil   d. Umbrella

111. ★★ What does the king say as you pass by the royal croquet game?

    a. "Rule 42, the queen always wins."

    b. "Rule 32, the queen always wins"

    c. "Rule 42, the queen never wins"

    d. "Rule 32, off with her head"

112. ★ What suit does the executioner card display when the queen says "Off With her Head"?

    a. Hearts   c. Diamonds

    b. Clubs   d. Spades

113. ★★ When you see the Unbirthday Party, what color is the cake in the center of the table?

a. Blue   c. Pink

b. Green   d. Yellow

114. ★★ As you walk toward the Matterhorn attraction, you will see a popcorn cart. What character is cranking the popcorn inside?

    a. Abominable Snowman

    b. Tinker Bell

    c. Cheshire Cat

    d. Mickey Mouse

115. ★ As you approach the Matterhorn Bobsled attraction, you will find a footprint displayed. What is the year on the brass plaque beneath the footprint?

    a. May 28, 1967   c. March 27, 1978

    b. May 27, 1978   d. May 27 1987

Matterhorn Bobsleds

Did you know?

The decades-old rumor of the existence of the half basketball court within the Matterhorn attraction is true. Although very few have had the privilege to see this hidden treasure, the court does in fact exist.

Did you know?

If you look up at the snowy top of the Matterhorn attraction you will see two very visible holes in the mountain. This was the access way for the Skyway attraction that took guests from Fantasyland to Tomorrowland and back. The attraction closed in 1999, but these tell-tale tunnels still remain.

It's a Small World

116. ★ As you approach the It's a Small World attraction, look at the sign above. How many children are there sailing in the boat?

    a. 12   c. 14
    b. 13   d. 15

117. ★★★ Before you board your boat, watch for the time display at the front of It's a Small World. How many children are there parading from the clock?

    a. 20   c. 30
    b. 24   d. 10

118. ★★ As you enter the introduction to It's a Small World, what color is the banner that reads, "sailed"?

    a. Pink   c. Yellow
    b. Green   d. Blue

119. ★ What creature is paddling the canoe in the North Pole scene?

    a. Koala   c. Walrus
    b. Penguin   d. Stork

120. ★ As you approach England, how many of the wooden soldiers are playing the drums?

    a. 9   c. 3
    b. 6   d. 12

121. ★★ As you enter France, what famous monument stands behind the can-can dancers?

    a. The Louvre   c. Eiffel Tower
    b. Versailles   d. Momont

122. ★★ As you continue your cruise, what country comes after Holland?

    a. Scotland   c. Italy
    b. France   d. Ireland

123. ★★ What shape are the pendulums of the cuckoo clocks in Switzerland?

    a. Hearts   c. Stars
    b. Circles   d. Triangles

124. ★★ As you explore the next scene, what famous animated couple flies high above you on a magic carpet?

    a. Belle and Beast   c. Aladdin and Jasmine
    b. Ariel and Eric   d. Mulan and Mushu

125. ★★ How many arms does the goddess statue in Thailand have?

    a. 2   c. 8
    b. 6   d. 4

126. ★★ As you approach China, which famous animated character adorns the kite Mulan holds?

    a. Mulan   c. Pumba
    b. Mushu   d. Tinker Bell

127. ★ What color is the elephant in the African continent?

    a. Pink   c. Grey
    b. Blue   d. Yellow

128. ★★★ As you continue cruising through Africa, how many dancers with red feathers do you see?

    a. 6   c. 8
    b. 10   d. 12

129. ★ As you enter South America, what do the penguins wear on their heads?

a. Feathers   c. Flowers

b. Sombreros   d. Top Hats

130. ★★ What musical instrument does the cactus play in South America?

a. Maracas   c. Tambourine

b. Guitar   d. Banjo

131. ★ What does the sign read as you approach Hawaii?

a. Aloha   c. Mele Kalikimaka

b. Welcome   d. Hawaiian Islands

132. ★★ Which animated characters are riding the surfboard in Hawaii?

a. Mickey and Minnie   c. Lilo and Nani

b. Donald and Daisy   d. Lilo and Stitch

133. ★ As you continue cruising Hawaii, what creatures fly high above your head?

a. Butterflies   c. Birds

b. Cranes   d. Bees

134. ★ What item is Woody holding in his hand as you enter the United States?

a. Gun   c. Guitar

b. Cowboy Hat   d. Lasso

135. ★ As you finish your cruise, what does the first postcard read as you enter the tunnel?

a. Wish you were here

b. Farewell

c. Weather's nice

d. Come back again

Snow White's Grotto

136. ★ If you look to the right of the castle, you will find a path to the Snow White wishing well. As you cross the bridge to this grotto, what shapes adorn the bridge fence?

a. Hearts   c. Diamonds

b. Flowers   d. Bunnies

137. ★★ While standing at the wishing well of Snow White grotto, what famous song do you hear being sung?

a. "When You Wish Upon a Star"

b. "I'm Wishing"

c. "Second Star to the Right"

d. "Heigh Ho"

138. ★ As you look at the wishing well, what forest creatures are carved into the support?

a. Bunnies   c. Owls

b. Squirrels   d. Deer

139. ★ As you turn to the figures of Snow White and the seven dwarves on the grotto, which dwarf stands guard at the front of the mine?

a. Dopey   c. Grumpy

b. Happy   d. Bashful

Did you know?

The marble statues of Snow White and the seven dwarves were mistakenly carved all the same size. Rather than redoing the Snow White statue, the imagineers created a forced perspective, putting Snow White at the top of the grotto so she appears larger than the dwarves below.

Fantasy Faire

140. ★ As you enter the Fantasy Faire, you will see a tower in the center of the courtyard. Which animated character sits atop this tower?

a. Sleeping Beauty   c. Snow White

b. Rapunzel   d. Jasmine

Did you know?

Next to the princess meeting area stands a shadow box of Clopin from *The Hunchback of Notre Dame*. As you crank the handle to hear the music and watch Clopin dance, look at the background characters. You will see many of the Disney character from other films hiding in the crowd.

141. ★★ Look at the reward poster for Flynn Rider. How much is the reward for his capture?

a. $1,000   c. $100,000

b. $5,000   d. $10,000

142. ★ As you walk toward the tunnel to Frontierland look up at the windows above. What color is the bird in the cage?

a. Blue   c. White

b. Yellow   d. Brown

143. ★ As you walk toward the tunnel to Frontierland, read some of the notices on your right. What does the missing cat enjoy doing?

a. Chasing Mice   c. Lying in the Sun

b. Bird Watching   d. Playing with Dogs

144. ★ How many years in a row have Maurice's treats won the blue medal ribbon?

a. 5   c. 2
b. 6   d. 3

145. ★ As you look at Clopin's poster, finish this line, "Laugh until your sides get _____ "

a. Sore   c. Store
b. More   d. Bored

Looking for hints on your way? Click here to find what you seek.

Toontown

Step through the portal to Mickey's Toontown where you become a citizen of this crazy city. Meet your favorite animated friends and visit the homes of Mickey, Minnie, Goofy, and Donald.

Having difficulty on your scavenger hunt? Click the link at the bottom of the chapter for hints to help you on your way.

1. ★ Stop for a moment to read the "Toontown" sign above you. According to the sign, what does BPOM stand for? "Benevolent and Protective Order of _____"
   a. Mickey
   b. Mouse
   c. Monstro
   d. Minnie

2. ★ What logo do you see on the "Optimist Intoonational" sign?

a. Mickey hand

c. A smile

b. Mickey ears

d. A frown

3. ★ As you walk through the tunnel into Toontown, you will find the historical landmark sign number 3 ½. Finish the Motto of Toontown: "Laughter is _____ you can hear"

a. Happiness

c. Rainbows

b. Smiles

d. Sunshine

4. ★★ As you begin exploring Toontown, you will find Goofy's Freeze. What number appears on the license plate on this trailer?

a. 55

c. 7

b. 71

d. 38

5. ★★ As you look at the roof of Goofy's Freeze, what winter sport does it appear Goofy was attempting?

a. Ski Jump

c. Dog Sledding

b. Ice Hockey

d. Speed Skating

6. ★★ What piece of sporting equipment is stuck on the front door of Goofy's trailer?

a. Tennis Ball

c. Hockey puck

b. Baseball

d. Basketball

Goofy's Playhouse

7. ★★★ As you look at Goofy's house you will notice his Mailbox is full. Which famous character is on the postmark of Goofy's letter?

a. Mickey Mouse   c. Donald Duck

b. Roger Rabbit   d. Minnie Mouse

8. ★★ As you approach Goofy's house in Toontown, take a look around his garden. What animal sits atop the scarecrow-Goofy in the garden?

a. Squirrel   c. Chipmunk

b. Crow   d. Mouse

9. ★ In Goofy's garden you will find a wooden basket filled with fruits and vegetables. Which of these is *not* found in the basket?

a. Carrots   c. Corn

b. Watermelon   d. Pumpkin

10. ★ As you continue up the path you will come across Goofy's laundry drying in the breeze. What number can you find on Goofy's swimsuit?

a. 6   c. 3

b. 5   d. 7

11. ★ As you walk into Goofy's house, stop for a moment and look at the light above your head. What makes up the shade of the light?

a. Strawberry jelly   c. Grape jelly

b. Peanut Butter   d. Mustard

12. ★ As you enter Goofy's house, look at the shark mounted on the wall. What item does it hold in its teeth?

a. Fishing pole   c. Christmas tree

b. Underwear   d. Anchor

13. ★★ As you look at Goofy's piano, what is the title of the sheet music?

a. Silly Scales in B   c. Silly Scales in G

b. Silly Scones in G   d. Silly Symphony

14. ★ As you look up to the second floor of Goofy's house, which of these household items is used as one of the railings?

a. Hammer   c. Milk bottle

b. Golf club   d. Soda bottle

15. ★ As you walk into the backyard of Goofy's house, what color is the polka dot umbrella on Goofy's roof?

a. Blue   c. Red

b. Green   d. Yellow

Donald Duck's Boat

16. ★ As you approach Donald Duck's house, what color is the flag on Donald's mailbox?

a. Red   c. Green

b. Blue   d. White

17. ★ What is the name of Donald's boat according to the rear of his house?

a. S.S. Donald   c. S.S. Daisy

b. Miss Daisy   d. S.S. Duck

18. ★ As you enter Donald's house, look at his bunk. How many pictures do you see hanging on the wall?

a. 3   c. 4

b. 5   d. 2

19. ★★ What kind of hat hangs on the wall in Donald's bunk?

a. Sombrero   c. Top hat

b. Sailor cap   d. Rain hat

20. ★★★ As you exit to the back of Donald's house, take a close look at the pylons around Donald's boat. Which sea creature is clinging to one of the posts?

a. Octopus c. Lobster

b. Starfish d. Crab

Gadget's Go Coaster

21. ★ As you look at the sign for Gadget's Go Coaster, what item make up the letter *A* in "Gadget"?

a. Ruler c. Spring

b. Magnet d. Hammer

22. ★ As you enter the queue for Gadget's Go Coaster, what nature item makes up the cars of the coaster?

a. Pea Pods c. Pinecones

b. Acorns d. Flowers

23. ★ As you pass over the first bridge in the queue for Gadget's Go Coaster, you will see the rungs made from match sticks. What is the railing on top made from?

a. Golf club c. Gardening rake

b. Walking stick d. Toothbrush

24. ★ As you cross the second bridge in the queue for Gadget's Go Coaster, what everyday item is used for the rungs on the bridge fence with the pencil railing?

a. Rubber bands c. Rulers

b. Deflated balloons d. Dental floss

25. ★ As you begin your approach to Gadget's house, what every-day item is used for the rain gutters on the outside of the house?

    a.   Drain pipes   c.   Drinking straws

    b.   Garden hose   d.   Pipe cleaners

26.   ★ As you enter the house for your coaster ride, what item makes up the doors on the gates of the queue?

    a.   Playing cards   c.   Cereal boxes

    b.   Dominoes   d.   Detergent boxes

27.   ★★ As you look across the loading queue, you will find a console with an eraser. What number is stamped in the lower left corner of the eraser?

    a.   19   c.   55

    b.   71   d.   05

28.   ★★ As you read the blueprints behind the pink eraser, what kind of soup does the label read on the can?

    a.   Tomato   c.   Pinecone

    b.   Asparagus   d.   Walnut

29.   ★★ As you look at the shelf above the blueprints, what object is used to hold the tools on the right?

    a.   Thimble   c.   Milk Bottle

    b.   Bucket   d.   Soup Bowl

30.   ★★★ As you look across at the blueprints for the coaster, what common item is used as a gear to attach the wheel?

    a.   Dime   c.   Nickel

    b.   Quarter   d.   Penny

31.   ★★ As you continue looking around the loading queue, you will find a set of blueprints stamped "Rejected." What is the name of the construction company written on these blueprints?

    a.   Acorn Acres   c.   Mickey Mouse

    b.   Chim Chim Cheree   d.   Chinny Chin Chin

32.   ★★ To the left of the loading queue, you will find a blueprint for the fences. What does the note below the scissors read?

a. Blade down

b. Do not run with

c. Danger, handle with care

d. This is dumb

33.   ★ To the left side of the queue, across from you is a console for the cast members, what object is this console made from?

a. Butter dish   c. Sardine can

b. Plastic tub   d. Espresso machine

34.   ★ On the front of the console to the left of the queue are power indicators. Which of these is *not* one of the power levels?

a. Max Power

b. Full Power

c. Extra Power

d. Whoa! Way too Much

35.   ★ As you exit Gadget's Go Coaster, look at the sign post as you exit. What substance is stuck to the spoon?

a. Honey   c. Jam

b. Peanut butter   d. Glue

Mickey Mouse House

36.   ★ As you enter the front door of Mickey's house, what company is the manufacturer of Pluto's doggie door?

a. Ace   c. Toon

b. Acme   d. Alpha

37.   ★★ As you look around the foyer, which of these items is *not* sticking out of Mickey's closet?

    a.   Tennis racket   c.   Shoe

    b.   Football   d.   Hockey stick

38.   ★★ As you enter the living room of Mickey's house, take a look at Mickey's radio. What is the last number on the far right on the dial?

    a.   1200   c.   530

    b.   1400   d.   900

39.   ★★ As you peek inside Mickey's bookcase, read the inscription on the baseball. Who gave the ball to Mickey?

    a.   Babe Ruth

    b.   Goofy

    c.   Toontown Little League

    d.   Fantasyland Little League

40.   ★ As you look around the house, take a peek at Mickey's desk. Which book lies on its side on the bookshelf?

    a.   Moby Duck   c.   The Smile Book

    b.   Cheese and Peace   d.   The Big Cheesy

41.   ★ As you read the papers of Mickey's desk, what is the sixth item on Mickey's "things to do" list?

    a.   Call Minnie   c.   Mousersize

    b.   Play with Pluto   d.   Water lawn

42.   ★★ If you look at Mickey's corkboard, who is getting married to Purnella Pullet?

    a.   Foghorn Leghorn   c.   Hick Rooster

    b.   Scrooge McDuck   d.   Ron Rooster

43.   ★★ According to the claim check, how many pairs of red shorts will Mickey pick up on Thursday?

a. 34   c. 12

b. 24   d. 32

44. ★ What company is the manufacturer of Mickey's piano?

a. Mouseway   c. Steinway

b. Henway   d. Mouswin

45. ★ Take a look at Pluto's bed next to the fireplace. What item sits in his bed?

a. Bone   c. Squeaky toy

b. Newspaper   d. Slipper

46. ★★ Look around this room carefully. How many darts do you see in the wall?

a. 3   c. 7

b. 4   d. 6

47. ★ What award is framed on the shelf above Pluto's bed in the family room?

a. Citizenship   c. Golf

b. Mice Skating   d. Dog Sledding

48. ★★ As you enter Mickey's laundry room, what does the product Toowny do?

a. Fabric hardener   c. Spot remover

b. Fabric softener   d. Bleach

49. ★ What month and year are displayed on the calendar in Mickey's laundry room?

a. July 1955   c. June 1971

b. February 1942   d. July 1942

50. ★★ What does the caption read on the picture on Mickey's calendar in the laundry room?

a. Plane Crazy   c. Valentine's Day

b. Steamboat Willie   d. Society Dog Show

51. ★ As you look at the drying laundry, where did Mickey get his red towel?

a. Tower Hotel
c. Toontown Hotel
b. Hiltoon Hotel
d. Disneyland Hotel

52. ★★ If you read the memo to the broom company, where does Mickey want them delivered?

a. Minnie's House
c. Goofy's House
b. The Movie Barn
d. Donald's House

53. ★ As you enter Mickey's barn, how many chickens are clucking at you?

a. 3
c. 7
b. 5
d. 2

54. ★ As you walk into the next room, take a look at the drawers on the wall. What does the long thin purple drawer contain?

a. Croc's cloaks
c. Ostrich feathers
b. Hippo's tutu's
d. Mickey's socks

55. ★★★ Exactly how many paint cans do you see in the Duck at Work area?

a. 25
c. 16
b. 31
d. 47

56. ★★ If you look up at the projection room, how did Goofy sign in for his shift?

a. His Name
c. Pawprint
b. An *X*
d. Yup

57. ★★ As you exit the film barn you will go through Mickey's garage. As you find Mickey's recyclables, which of these is *not* one of the cans?

a. Cans   c. Paper

b. Glass   d. Gloves

Minnie Mouse House

58. ★★ As you enter Minnie's house, you will find her radio in the living room. Between which numbers is the dial set?

a. 60 – 70   c. 120 – 160

b. 54 – 60   d. 90 – 120

59. ★ As you look at Minnie's easy chair, what catalog sits on the arm of her chair?

a. Victoria's Secret   c. Jessica's Secret

b. Minnie's Secret   d. Daisy's Secret

60. ★ As you look at Minnie's knitting basket, what color yarn is sitting with her needles?

a. Green   c. Blue

b. Red   d. White

61. ★★ As you look around the living room, notice Minnie's bookshelf. What author wrote *Cheese and Remembrance*?

a. Herman Mouse   c. Jerry Mouse

b. Mickey Mouse   d. Mortimer Mouse

62. ★★★ Listen to the messages on Minnie's answering machine. Why does Mickey break their date for tonight?

a. He has another date

b. Goofy needs help at the bar

c. Pluto ran away

d. He is very busy at the movie barn

63. ★ As you enter Minnie's kitchen, what is the brand name of her refrigerator?

a. Toonmore   c. Cheesemore

b. Mickeymore   d. Fridgemore

64. ★★ According to Minnie's cookie recipe on the front of her refrigerator, how many ounces of cheese chips are required?

a. 8 oz   c. 6 oz

b. 10 oz   d. 2 oz

65. ★★ What is the seventeenth item on Minnie's shopping list?

a. Gouda   c. Cheese Cake

b. Sharp Cheddar   d. Mouserella

Did you know?

If you turn the knobs on Minnie's stove, watch the glass. Her cake will rise as it bakes and then fall again.

---

66. ★ Look at the yummy cookies on Minnie's kitchen table. According to the accompanying note, what makes them special?

a. They're diet

b. They're made with love

c. They're for Mickey

d. They're for you

67. ★ As you examine Minnie's stove, what item sits on top next to the kitchen timer?

a. Salt shaker   c. Sugar

b. Baking soda   d. Flour

68. ★ Minnie has many kitchen items on the shelves around the kitchen. What shape are her salt and pepper shakers?

a. Hearts   c. Frogs

b. Flowers   d. Cheese

69. ★★ As you see Minnie's canisters on the kitchen counter, which of these is *not* one of the canister labels?

a. Nuts   c. Cheese

b. Candy   d. Cookies

70. ★ As you exit Minnie's house and continue walking through Toontown, notice the road sign across the street from Minnie's. Which direction does this sign indicate?

a. Right Turn   c. U Turn

b. Left Turn   d. Wrong Turn

71. ★★ To your left are the Toontown restrooms. Which famous character adorns the sign for the ladies room?

a. Minnie Mouse   c. Daisy Duck

b. Jessica Rabbit   d. Clara Cluck

72. ★★ As you approach Goofy's gas station, you will see a car waiting for service. As you look at the luggage, what item of clothing is sticking out?

a. Sock   c. Scarf

b. Shoe   d. Tie

73. ★ As you explore Goofy's gas station, according to the sign how do you ask for service?

a. Scream   c. Dance

b. Honk   d. Sing

74. ★ As you explore Goofy's gas station, according to the signs, what is free?

a. Gas   c. Oil

b. Water   d. Air

75. ★ You will see a dog house at Goofy's gas station. What is the name on this dog house?

   a. Fifi
   b. Pluto
   c. Bruiser
   d. Spike

76. ★ As you read the sign for Goofy's water, which of these is *not* one of the flavor's available?

   a. Zippy Water
   b. Loopy Water
   c. Dry Water
   d. Whacky Water

77. ★★ What is the name of the bank you encounter as you continue your tour of Toontown?

   a. Toontown 1st National
   b. Mickey's Bank
   c. Toontown Piggybank
   d. 3rd Little Piggy

78. ★ As you look at the doors of the bank, what do you break in case of emergency?

   a. Pig
   b. Doors
   c. Glass
   d. Bank

79. ★★ As you approach the courthouse, read the window. Which Toontown citizen is the investment counselor?

   a. Roger Rabbit
   b. Scrooge McDuck
   c. Mickey Mouse
   d. Goofy

80. ★★ What year is displayed on the official seal of Toontown?

   a. 1955
   b. 1971
   c. 1928
   d. 1988

81. ★ As you continue looking at the windows around the courthouse, what business stands next to the Toontown schoolhouse?

a. Ink and Paint

b. Toontown Post Office

c. Laugh O' Gram Films

d. Glass Factory

82. ★★ As you come to the Toontown Five and Dime store, enter the store and take a look around at the shelf above you. What color is the tail sticking out of the Shaggy Dog box?

a. Brown

b. Gray

c. Red

d. Black

83. ★★ What household item rests in front of the barrel marked "Fragile"?

a. Hammer

b. Hair dryer

c. Mouse trap

d. Rubber chicken

84. ★★ As you continue your search around the Five and Dime, what is written on the spool of wire next to the Tall Tales box?

a. One Liners

b. Wire

c. Extra spool

d. Do not touch

85. ★★ According to the crate above your head, who will the singing harp be delivered to?

a. Mickey Mouse

b. Donald Duck

c. Goofy

d. W. Giant

86. ★★ Look very closely at the wall to the right of the singing harp. What are you warned not to do to the wall?

a. Park

b. Paint

c. Enter

d. Knock

87.   ★★ As you exit the store, look up at the marquee for the Laugh Factory. What is the fifth level of laughter from left to right?

a.   Guffaw   c.   Chuckle

b.   Smirk   d.   Giggle

88.   ★★ Across from the Laugh Factory, you will find a doorbell shaped like a cat. What sound do you hear when you push the bell?

a.   Bell   c.   Meow

b.   Bark   d.   Moo

Did you know?
If you look to your left you will find the Toontown Power Company. When you open the door you may receive the shock of your life.

Did you know?
Find the red doorbell for the glass factory, but be careful, you might shatter the contents inside. You can also open the tops of the boxes to hear various sounds from all over Toontown.

Did you know?
At the Fireworks factory, pull the plunger on the ground in front of the building. Push down on the plunger more than once to hear the various sounds coming from the building.

89.   ★★ Around the corner from the Fireworks factory, you will find the Toontown post office. Which of these is *not* one of the post office boxes you see for the Toontown residents?

a.   Mickey Mouse   c.   Jessica Rabbit

b.   Chip and Dale   d.   Goofy

90.   ★ Within the Toontown post office, the clerk is *not* in. What does the sign say on the window?

    a.   Gone Fishing   c.   Out of my Mind

    b.   Gone to Lunch   d.   Gone Home

91.   ★★ As you approach Roger Rabbit's Cartoon Spin, the Toontown insurance agency is next door. Which of these is *not* one of the accidents they insure?

    a.   Falling off cliffs

    b.   Explosions

    c.   Falling down rabbit holes

    d.   Getting run over by steamrollers

Roger Rabbit's Cartoon Spin

92.   ★★ As you enter Roger Rabbit's Cartoon Spin, look at the wall to your right. Which of these license plates on the wall would the White Rabbit from *Alice in Wonderland* use?

    a.   BB WOLF   c.   1D N PTR

    b.   1DRLND   d.   IM L8

93.   ★★★ Which of the license plates on the wall would be used in Song of the South?

    a.   ZPD2DA   c.   RS2CAT

    b.   FAN TC   d.   CAP 10 HK

94.   ★ As you begin your adventure through the queue for Roger Rabbit's Cartoon Spin, what is the speed limit for the road?

    a.   50   c.   30

    b.   40   d.   25

95. ★ As you continue into the queue for Roger Rabbit's Cartoon Spin, take a look at the call board. Which of these is *not* one of the call times on the chalkboard?

    a.   9 pm   c.   11:45

    b.   10:30 pm   d.   Midnight

96. ★ According to the call board, which act is number four on the list?

    a.   Card tricks   c.   Dog tricks

    b.   Ballet   d.   Finale

97. ★★ Within the prop cage, you will find various item used on the stage. How many pies do you find?

    a.   4   c.   3

    b.   6   d.   5

98. ★ As you read the audition board across from the prop cage, which of these is *not* welcome at the Tuesday audition?

    a.   Men   c.   Giants

    b.   Women   d.   Animals

99. ★★ As you walk past the prop cage and into the next room look carefully around you. What does the warning sign ask you to do?

    a.   Travel in pairs   c.   Travel fast

    b.   Travel alone   d.   Watch carefully

100. ★ As you enter the Dip room, which of these is *not* one of the ingredients for Dip?

a. Fluorine

b. Acetone

c. Benzene

d. Turpentine

101. ★★ As you pass by Baby Herman's dressing room look around the room. Which of these items does *not* appear on his table?

a. Cigars

b. Television

c. Onions

d. Liver

102. ★★ What time does the clock in Baby Herman's dressing room display?

a. 7:05

b. 12:30

c. 8:05

d. 2:45

103. ★★★ As you come to the loading area, look at the area across from the loading zone. How many darts are in the dartboard?

a. 5

b. 7

c. 3

d. 2

104. ★ As you begin your journey into Toontown, which character is tied up in the trunk of the weasel's car?

a. Roger Rabbit

b. Jessica Rabbit

c. Bennie

d. Mickey Mouse

105. ★★ As you exit the china shop, what does the street sign read as you pass by?

a. Spin

b. Stop

c. Go

d. Yield

106. ★★ As you pass by the grocery store, what does the sign in the window advertise?

    a.   Poison Apples

    b.   Wishing Apples

    c.   Golden Apples

    d.   Granny Smith Apples

107. ★ As you travel through the Power House, what does the warning sign on the wall say?

a.	Keep Out	c.	Stand Clear
b.	Wet Floor	d.	Wrong Way

108. ★★ As you see Roger and the Weasel, what is the weasel wearing as he holds onto Roger?

a.	Sweater	c.	Trench coat
b.	Beanie	d.	Straight jacket

109. ★★★ As you go through the explosion and begin falling, what theoretical theorem do you see spinning past you?

    a. $E=MC2$

    b. $A2 + B2 = C2$

    c.   3.14

    d. $Y = B2 +- 4 \times A \times C$

110. ★★ As you enter the Gag Factory, what does the box behind the clown punching bag contain?

a.	Anvils	c.	Rubber wieners
b.	Rubber chickens	d.	Cuckoo clocks

111. ★★★ Keep a sharp eye out for the tap-dancing shoes. How many pairs of shoes do you see?

a.	1	c.	6
b.	4	d.	10

112. ★ As you pass by the jack-in-the-boxes, what letter adorns the blue box?

a. J   c. W

b. C   d. K

113. ★ As you pass by Jessica with the sledge hammer, what do you see circling the weasel's head that she has hit?

    a. Tweeting birds   c. Hearts

    b. Questions marks   d. Stars

114. ★ What animal do you see hung above you as you turn the corner of the boxes?

    a. Kangaroo   c. Weasel

    b. Elephant   d. Giraffe

115. ★★★ As you exit your ride vehicle, take once last look at the desk across from you. What does the framed certificate in the lower right corner state?

    a. Mr. Tailpipe   c. Mr. Wrench

    b. Mr. Screwdriver   d. Mr. Firestone

116. ★★★ As you look at the dispatchers desk, which of these is *not* one of the items you will see on the desk?

    a. Telephone   c. Stapler

    b. Radio   d. Coffee Thermos

Looking for hints on your way? Click here to find what you seek.

Adventureland

Take some time to explore the far-off exotic places Adventureland has to offer. Investigate the jungle or explore a temple. Only the limits of your imagination will hold you back from the adventure around the next corner.

Having difficulty on your scavenger hunt? Click the link at the bottom of the chapter for hints to help you on your way.

Did you know?
When Adventureland first opened, Walt Disney opened a restaurant that featured authentic Polynesian food and dancers.

1.   ★ As you enter Adventureland, look up at the sign above you. What material are the letters spelling Adventureland made from?

a.   Reeds   c.   Wood

b.   Bamboo   d.   Grass

2.   ★ As you look to your left and right you will notice the gates of Adventureland adorned with shields, spears and various items from the islands. How many skulls do you find?

a.   3   c.   4

b.   5   d.   7

3.   ★ As you cross the bridge to Adventureland, you will notice the restrooms before you. As you look up, what animal symbol adorns the building just below the eaves?

a.   Tiger   c.   Alligator

b.   Lion   d.   Eagle

4.   ★ As you enter the Adventureland Bazaar, you will see an alcove at the rear of the store. Aladdin's Other Lamp is found in this area. As you read the tapestry above, finish this line, "Receive the wisdom of the Genie and have their _____ revealed."

a.   Future   c.   Destiny

b.   Fortune   d.   Freedom

5.   ★★★ In the center of this store, you will find Rajah's Mint. How many coins do you find around the base of Rajah's Mint?

a.   35   c.   56

b.   72   d.   32

6. ★ As you enter the South Seas Traders shop in Adventureland, the sign on the right side of the cash register stand reads, "Assorted Tropical Fruit, Do Not _____."

   a. Pick   c. Ship

   b. Open   d. Freeze

Did you know?

In the center of this store is Shrunken Ned displayed in his glass case. Place your coin in the slot to hear his wisdom and receive your fortune card.

7. ★ According to the sign at the back of the South Seas Trader shop, what sort of rental is available at the south dock?

   a. Boats   c. Inner tubes

   b. Surfboards   d. Fishing gear

8. ★ According to the Caribe Ferry sign to the right of the cash register stand, which of these is *not* one of the ports of call?

   a. Antigua   c. Martinique

   b. Tortuga   d. Tortola

Did you know?

If you look above the cash register stand in the South Seas Trader shop, you will find a live bird in a cage. The cast members keep a bird as a pet mascot for this store.

you enter the Indiana Jones Outpost shop, the wooden crates making up the cash register stan. According to the shipping label, where can Mr. Livingston be found?

a. Somewhere in the Amazon

b. Somewhere on the Jungle Cruise

c. Somewhere in The Nile

d. Somewhere in the Congo

10. ★★ If you read the labels on the crates carefully, what item is being shipped with the Quinine Tablets?

a. Mosquito nets   c. Coconuts

b. Ammunition   d. Elephant guns

11. ★★ As you exit the Indiana Jones Outpost shop, look at the wall to your right. You will notice a series of animal sculptures on the wall next to the Bengal Barbeque. Which of these is *not* one you will see?

a. Lizard   c. Lion

b. Elephant   d. Gorilla

The Enchanted Tiki Room

12. ★★ As you enter the queue for the Enchanted Tiki Room, look to the left of the turnstile. Which native god greets you?

a. Maui   c. Pele

b. Koro   d. Tangaroa-Ru

13. ★★ As each of the island gods are introduced to you, the Goddess Pele rules over fire and what?

a. Water   c. Volcanoes

b. Sand   d. Islands

· ·

Did you know?

As you walk up the steps to the Tiki room, you will notice hidden bathrooms. This is one of the best-kept secrets at Disneyland. They are useful on a busy day, and very few guests are aware of these hidden gems.

· ·

Bonus Question

14. ★★★ Since we are on the subject of Disneyland bathrooms, how many bathrooms are there total inside Disneyland?

    a.   13   c.   12

    b.   14   d.   16

15. ★ As the Tiki Room show begins, which of these is *not* one of the hosts names?

    a.   Frederick   c.   Fritz

    b.   Jose   d.   Pierre

16. ★★ According to the song, if the birds were not in the show, where would they be?

    a.   Out the Door   c.   Flying away

    b.   In the Audience   d.   Riding the tea cups

17. ★★ According to your Emcee, what is Fritz missing?

    a.   Feathers   c.   Hair

    b.   Wings   d.   Tail

18. ★★ Which of these is *not* one of the names of the white birds on the bird mobile?

    a.   Collette   c.   Gigi

    b.   Fifi   d.   Juanita

19. ★★ Jose wonders aloud what happened to which bird?

    a.   Rosita   c.   Maria

    b.   Juanita   d.   Tatiana

20. ★★ What kind of flowers, found in the corners of the room, sing a Hawaiian song?

    a.   Roses   c.   Hydrangea

    b.   Birds of Paradise   d.   Daisies

21. ★ When the rain begins, what does Fritz say has been left running?

    a.   The shower   c.   The faucet

    b.   The hose   d.   The river

22. ★ When the thunder begins, who do the birds say is angered by all the celebrating?

    a.   The volcano   c.   The gods

    b.   The tikis   d.   The birds

23. ★★ What famous Disney song is heard as you exit the Enchanted Tiki Room?

    a.   "Zip A dee Do Dah"

    b.   "Mickey Mouse Club"

    c.   "Heigh Ho"

    d.   "It's a Small World"

The Jungle Cruise

24. ★ Before you enter the Jungle Cruise queue, look at the outer wall to your left. Which of these is *not* one of the listed items in stock?

    a.   Provisions   c.   Ammunition

    b.   Fuel   d.   Water

25. ★ As you enter the queue for The Jungle Cruise, take a look at the advertisement on the wall to your left. What year was Jungle Navigation established?

   a. 1955   c. 1921
   b. 1971   d. 1911

26. ★ As you enter the queue for The Jungle Cruise, take a look at the advertisement on the wall to your left. What city follows Zanzibar?

   a. Anaheim   c. Orlando
   b. Calcutta   d. Cairo

27. ★★ As you continue through The Jungle Cruise queue, what airline is advertised on the poster next to the ticket window?

   a. Air Africa   c. Air Afrique
   b. Air Morocco   d. Air Avion

28. ★★★ Which of these is *not* one of the rivers you explore on the Jungle Cruise?

   a. Amazon   c. Nile
   b. Ganges   d. Congo

29. ★ As you enter the boat for your Jungle Cruise adventure, what name is in the heart carved in the boat next to your skipper?

   a. Pat   c. Jill
   b. Cat   d. Pam

30. ★★ As you begin your cruise, you will enter the sacred shrine. According to your skipper, what is the name of the crocodile you see to the left of your boat in the water?

   a. Snappy   c. Cinnamon
   b. Dundee   d. Ginger

31. ★★★ As you enter the sacred elephant bathing pool, how many elephants do you see?

a. 17
c. 12
b. 16
d. 7

32. ★ According to your skipper, why is taking photos permitted in the elephant bathing pool?

a. You have a permit
b. They have their trunks on
c. You are on a reserve
d. The group is safe

33. ★ According to your skipper, what is the name of the elephant in the shower?

a. Bertha
c. Mrs. Jumbo
b. Dumbo
d. Bert

34. ★ As you pass by the gorilla reaching for his bananas, what additional item sits atop the crate in the water?

a. Apples
c. Lantern
b. Sack of Flour
d. Gas can

35. ★★ According to your skipper, who were the falls named after?

a. Albert Schweitzer
c. Albert Einstein
b. Albert Falls
d. Albert Brooks

36. ★ According to your skipper, which river is the longest in the world?

a. The Congo
c. The Nile
b. The Amazon
d. The Ganges

37. ★★ As you enter the African belt, how many vultures are watching over the pride of lions in their den?

a. 5   c. 3

b. 6   d. 8

38. ★ As you encounter the exploration party climbing the pole, what kind of animal is watching from the river bank?

a. Lions   c. Zebras

b. Tigers   d. Hyenas

39. ★★ As you enter the hippo pool, how do you know the hippos are about to attack, according to your skipper?

a. Roaring   c. Shooting a pistol

b. Wiggling their ears   d. Singing

40. ★ As you approach the native camp, what items are stacked inside the canoe at the river edge?

a. Paddles   c. Skulls

b. Spears   d. Shields

41. ★ As you pass the native village, what do the ambush party hold in their hands?

a. Blow guns   c. Pistols

b. Daggers   d. Spears

42. ★ According to your skipper, what is the eighth wonder of the world?

a. The Elephant Bathing Pool

b. The African Belt

c. Civilization

d. The Back Side of Water

43. ★ As you pass by the Piranha pool, what type of snake is sitting in the tree?

a. Python   c. Rattlesnake

b. Cobra   d. Cottonmouth

51. ★★ As you watch the film on safety tips for your journey, which *Indiana Jones* character is narrating?

a. Indiana Jones   c. Marion

b. Sallah   d. Marcus Brody

52. ★★ As you watch the film, what item does the boy put into the pouch in the vehicle?

a. Pocket Knife   c. Backpack

b. Blowgun   d. Slingshot

53. ★ As your narrator continues the safety warnings, what does the sign he hold say?

a. Take Heed   c. Safety Tips

b. Be Warned   d. Temple Treasures

54. ★ As you finish watching the safety clip, what is the name of the news company?

a. Eye on the World   c. Eye on the Glass

b. Eye on the Future   d. Eye on the Globe

55. ★★★ As you enter the next small room, notice the cage to your right, according to the small stamp, where does it say to deliver to?

a. Club Jones   c. Club Lucas

b. Club Obi Wan   d. Club Harrison

56. ★★ As you walk up the incline, you will see several crates. According to the stamp, how many dozen bottles are in the crate?

a. 10
c. 15
b. 13
d. 12

57. ★★ Just before you begin your ascent up the stairs, you will notice an elevator to your left. What words are stamped on the inner wall of the elevator?

a. Freight
c. Wall Moves
b. Danger
d. Falling Rocks

58. ★ As you enter your ride vehicle and begin your adventure, what common object do you see on the wall to your left just before your first turn?

a. Mirrors
c. Camping Gear
b. Coffee Pots
d. Flower Pots

59. ★ As you begin your journey, what does your guide tell you need a little adjusting?

a. Seats
c. Maps
b. Mirrors
d. Brakes

60. ★★ As you choose your destiny, which of these is *not* one of the paths you can take?

a. Riches
c. Youth
b. Beauty
d. Future

61. ★ As you see the idol of Mara and look into her eyes, where does she say your destiny lies?

a. Beyond the Gates of Hades
b. Beyond the Ends of the Earth
c. Beyond the Gates of Doom
d. Beyond the Gates of the Temple

62. ★★ As you see Indiana Jones trying to close the gates, what does he tell you to do?
    a. Swerve left
    b. Swerve right
    c. Watch where you're going
    d. Look out

63. ★★★ As you enter the mummy room, how many times do the skeletons jump out at you?
    a. 2   c. 5
    b. 4   d. 3

64. ★★ As you cross the bridge and see the giant snake, what species of snake is attacking?
    a. Python   c. Cobra
    b. Rattlesnake   d. Cottonmouth

65. ★ As you are facing the giant snake, what do you hear Indiana Jones say?
    a. Snakes! I'm Out of Here!
    b. Snakes! Why did it have to be snakes?
    c. Snakes! no Snakes!
    d. Snake! You're on your own!

66. ★ As you enter the corridor where the giant guards stand on either side of you, what do they hold in their hands?
    a. Spears
    b. Blow Guns
    c. Arrows
    d. Whips

67. ★ As you exit your ride vehicle, look at the wall to your left. Which of these is *not* one of the carvings at the bottom of the inscription?

a. Snake

c. Skull

b. Gold pieces

d. Beetle

68. ★ As you exit your adventure, finish the inscription on the wooden box above your head and you exit the temple. "Real rewards await those who choose _____."

a. Carefully

c. Wisely

b. Intellectually

d. Cleverly

69. ★ As you come back into the light, what words are written on the large tank in the camp?

a. Distilled Water

c. Caution Hot

b. Hot Water

d. Drinking Water

70. ★★ As you continue along the path, you will see a large vehicle. As you look inside, what famous magazine do you see on the board inside?

a. *Time*

c. *Photoplay*

b. *Newsweek*

d. *Life*

Tarzan's Treehouse

71. ★ As you walk the steps of Tarzan's Treehouse you will come upon a warning sign. What does this sign say?

hy Way   c.   Mind Thy Head

hy Step   d.   Warning Turn Ba

72.   ★ As you come upon the first book, who was the author of the Tarzan stories?

a.   Edgar Rice Burroughs

b.   Jules Verne

c.   Edgar Allan Poe

d.   C.S. Lewis

73.   ★ As you approach the spot where the Jaguar is perched to attack, what item is seen in the slightly opened chest to the right of this creature?

a.   Books   c.   Leather

b.   Shoes   d.   Lace

Did you know?

If you stand in this area you will hear the growl of the Jaguar. Now look across at the cradle supported by the tree branches. You can hear a baby Tarzan crying.

74.   ★ As you continue your journey, what is the name of Tarzan's gorilla mother, according to the story books?

a.   Mara   c.   Kara

b.   Kala   d.   Mala

75.   ★ As you arrive at the room where Tarzan and his mother look in the mirror, touch the brass features on the book in front of you. Which of these does *not* appear in the mirror?

a.   The gorilla family members

b.   Tarzan's parents

c. Tarzan as he grows up

d. Your reflection

76. ★★★ As you look to the vanity table to your left, what does the black label on the bottle read?

a. Red Lion

c. Green Toadstool

b. Blue Otter

d. Amber Lion

77. ★ As you look at the table behind you next to the ships wheel, which of these is *not* one of the book colors you see?

a. Red

c. Yellow

b. Green

d. Blue

78. ★ As you arrive at the room where Tarzan and Jane are seen, what was Jane's first reaction to Tarzan according to the open book you find?

a. Fear

c. Curiosity

b. Excitement

d. Sadness

79. ★ As you look as the figure of Jane, what does she hold in her hand?

a. Tea cup

c. Quill

b. Book

d. Glove

80. ★ As you reach the camp at the base of the tree you will notice the old-fashioned record player. What color is the bell on this device?

a. Green

c. Red

b. Blue

d. Yellow

81. ★★ As you look around the camp, which two animated characters are hidden among the supplies?

a. Lilo and Stitch

b. Cogsworth and Lumiere

    c.   Mrs. Potts and Chip

    d.   Dumbo and Timothy

82.   ★★ As you look at the stove in the camp, what name appears on the bellows?

    a.   Superior   c.   Fantastic

    b.   Marvelous   d.   Ultimate

Bonus question:

83.   ★★★ How many stairs in total did you walk during your time on Tarzan's Treehouse including the tree-house and the camp?

    a.   120   c.   173

    b.   150   d.   137

Looking for hints on your way? Click here to find what you seek.

Frontierland

Go back to the days of the wild west and explore the roots of America with Cowboys and Indians. Take a wild ride on a runaway mine train or get up close and personal with live animals as you explore the origins of the United States.

Having difficulty on your scavenger hunt? Click the link at the bottom of the chapter for hints to help you on your way.

1.   ★ As you enter the fort gates of Frontierland, stop for a moment to read the inscriptions on the gates. According to the inscription, which war were the thirteen flags carried in?

a. Mexican-American   c. World War I

b. Civil   d. Revolutionary

2. ★★ In what year was the flag with "Don't Tread on Me" carried by soldiers?

a. 1776   c. 1864

b. 1775   d. 1971

3. ★ According to the inscription on the right gate of Frontierland, what was a parapet?

a. Fire Step   c. Rain Step

b. Water Step   d. House Step

4. ★ According to the right gate inscription, which of these is *not* one of the forts listed?

a. Ft. Pitt   c. Ft. Mimms

b. Ft. Bragg   d. Ft. Harrod

5. ★ As you look across at the building to the right, what do you see resting on the roof of this building?

a. Animal pelts   c. Antlers

b. Shotguns   d. Baskets

6. ★ To your left, you will find the Pioneer Mercantile. In what year was this store established?

a. 1955   c. 1864

b. 1971   d. 1807

Did you know?

If you look at the base of the flag pole you will find a bronze plaque given by the American Humane Society to Walt Disney for his humane ideals to people throughout the world dedicated July 1955.

Westward Ho Trading Company

7. ★★ As you enter the Westward Ho Trading Company, look at all of the pioneer artifacts around the shelves above your head. If you look directly to your left, what shape is the large cookie cutter above the Chesapeake boxes?

   a. Star

   b. Heart

   c. Circle

   d. Tree

8. ★ According to the label of the Steamship canisters, what sort of candy flavor do they make?

   a. Peppermint

   b. Toffee

   c. Molasses

   d. Taffy

9. ★ As you continue exploring the store, take a look at the old west artifacts on the shelves above your head. What product does the Morning Glory Brand make?

   a. Flour

   b. Sugar

   c. Tobacco

   d. Lard

Shooting Exposition

10. ★ As you exit the store, walk toward the Frontierland Shooting Exposition. According to Old Tom Hubbards grave, what did he die with?

    a. A Smile

    b. A Fortune

    c. A Frown

    d. A Clown

11. ★★ What is the date of Red Eye Dan's death, according to his tombstone?

    a. July 17

    b. August 14

    c. March 2

    d. December 21

12. ★ According to his tombstone, how many claims did Billy Jack jump?

    a. 5   c. 3

    b. 6   d. 12

13. ★ According to the epitaph, what do you see protruding from the grave of A. Carpenter?

    a. Saw   c. Screwdriver

    b. Hammer   d. Shovel

14. ★★ As you see the town in the distance, what is the name of the bank?

    a. Big Bucks   c. Short Change

    b. Frontierland   d. Deadwood

15. ★★ If you look at the large tree in the Boot Hills cemetery, how many vultures do you see?

    a. 3   c. 7

    b. 5   d. 1

Pioneer Mercantile

16. ★★ As you walk up to the Pioneer Mercantile in Frontierland, observe the entrance of this shop. How many oil lanterns do you see above your head?

    a. 14   c. 8

    b. 10   d. 24

17. ★★★ As you enter the Pioneer Mercantile, find the Woody's Ho-Down machine. What famous song plays as you make Woody dance?

    a. "Cowboy Serenade"

    b. "Woody's Round Up"

    c.   "I've got Spurs"

    d.   "Just Around the Riverbend"

18.   ★ As you make your way around the Pioneer Mercantile, what famous couple adorn the animal skin portrait above one of the cash register areas?

    a.   Woody and Jessie

    b.   Mickey and Minnie Mouse

    c.   Pocanhontas and John Smith

    d.   Tarzan and Jane

Did you know?

As you watch the classic western cartoon shorts on the screen at the back of the shop, look at the large Native American drum on the ceiling. This décor cleverly hides the video equipment, maintaining the ambiance of the store for the enjoyment of guests.

---

19.   ★★ As you continue through the shop, you will find an entrance to the Bonanza Outfitters. As you observe the western objects on the shelves, find the antique clothing dryer. What company manufactures this unique item?

    a.   General Mills   c.   Barnum

    b.   Quaker   d.   American Wringer

20.   ★ Behind the large counter between Bonanza Outfitters and Silver Spur Supplies, read the notice for the Pony Express. In how many days do the couriers need to go from Missouri to California?

    a.   7 days   c.   10 days

    b.   8 days   d.   15 days

21. ★ Behind this large counter read the warning letter. Which of these is *not* one of the outlaws listed?

    a. Bank robbers   c. Thieves

    b. Fakiers   d. Bunko-steerers

22. ★★ As you read the plate on the front of the safe behind this counter, in what city was it manufactured?

    a. Kansas City   c. Tombstone

    b. Dodge City   d. Birmingham

23. ★★★ What do the cast members keep inside of the safe behind the Bonanza Outfitters counter?

    a. Gold coins   c. Money bag

    b. Wooden coins   d. Gold nuggets

24. ★ As you enter Silver Spur Supplies, what outdoor sport item is suspended from the ceiling?

    a. Row boat   c. Hay wagon

    b. Canoe   d. Raft

25. ★ As you look above the cash register area, what does the sign say they buy and sell at top prices?

    a. Hides   c. Cattle

    b. Gold   d. Clothing

26. ★★ Notice the staircase leading to the second floor. How many stars adorn the stairs total?

    a. 60   c. 90

    b. 75   d. 120

27. ★★ As you look at the portraits of some of the famous Wild West residents, which of these is *not* one of the celebrities presented on the wall?

    a. Buffalo Bill Cody   c. John Wesley Hardin

    b. Calamity Jane   d. Wild Bill Hickok

28. ★★★ As you exit the shops and come back out to Frontierland, take a look at the signs above the stores. According to the Bonanza Outfitters, which of these is *not* one of the items they sell?

    a. Leather jackets   c. Vests

    b. Children's wear   d. Novelty wear

29. ★★ As you read the signs on the buildings, which of these names is partnered with Crockett on the hat company?

    a. Hickok   c. Woody

    b. Cody   d. Russel

Did you know?

As you walk the streets of Frontierland, notice the ground beneath your feet. Imprinted on the ground are images of horse shoes, boots, and wagon ruts, showing the residents of Frontierland moving around the town.

Golden Horseshoe

30. ★ As you continue your way through Frontierland, you will come across the Golden Horseshoe. As you read the posters in front of the theater, which of these acts comes from the east?

    a. Singers   c. Comedians

    b. Dancers   d. Acrobats

31. ★ According to the advertisements outside the Golden Horseshoe, what is provided for the ladies?

    a. Linen tablecloths   c. Powder rooms

    b. Clean glasses   d. Crystal stemware

32. ★ According to the advertisements outside the Golden Horseshoe, which of these is *not* one of the items not allowed inside?

   a. Cussing
   c. Ladies
   b. Animals
   d. Gun fighting

33. ★ As you look up at the marquee outside the entrance to the Golden Horseshoe, how many red stones adorn the horseshoe?

   a. 10
   c. 13
   b. 12
   d. 14

34. ★★ As you enter the Golden Horseshoe, notice the etched glass inside the entrance. What animal does Slue Foot Sue ride on the etched glass?

   a. Horse
   c. Ram
   b. Bull
   d. Fish

Did you know?

As you enter the Golden Horseshoe, look up at the box on the second floor to your left. This private box was where Walt Disney sat when he watched the shows. It remains waiting for Walt Disney to this day as guests are not allowed inside.

35. ★ As you look around the Golden Horseshoe, notice the bull horns around the room. How many set of horns do you see?

   a. 13
   c. 10
   b. 21
   d. 17

36.   ★★★ As you look at the Golden Horseshoe stage when
the curtain is open, read the advertisements. What is the
name of the head mistress of the finishing school?

a.   Miss Funicello   c.   Miss Taylor
b.   Miss Mouse   d.   Miss Daisy

37.   ★★★ According to the advertisements on the stage
curtain, where do Boag's Beans come from?

a.   New York   c.   Frontierland
b.   Chicago   d.   Kansas City

38.   ★★ As you look behind the bar at the Golden Horseshoe,
what does the barrel with the bull painted on the front
contain?

a.   Whiskey   c.   Lemonade
b.   Beer   d.   Root beer

• • • • • • • • • • • • • • • •

39.   ★ As you exit the Golden Horseshoe and walk around
the corner toward the Stage Door café, take a look at
the Laod Bhang fireworks mural. In what year was it
established?

a.   1955
b.   1971
c.   1854
d.   1845

Did you know?

As you walk toward the Rivers of America you will find a five-ton petrified redwood tree on display. There is a long-standing myth that Walt gave this tree to Lillian on their anniversary and she donated it to the park as it was too big for their home. This is in fact not correct as Walt Disney purchased the large fossil and joked to his family about it being an anniversary gift for many years. This was never fact and Walt Disney used the story as an ongoing gag throughout his life.

Mark Twain Riverboat

Did you know?

The Mark Twain Riverboat had her maiden voyage actually four days before Disneyland opened to the public. Walt and Lillian Disney celebrated their wedding anniversary on July 13, 1955 with a party aboard the Mark Twain for their close friends and family.

Did you know?

If you ask the cast members, you will be given permission to ride in the wheel-house with the captain of the Mark Twain.

40. ★★ As you listen to your narrator tell you about your journey, which of these is *not* one of the rivers you will visit?

a. Mississippi   c. Potomac

b. Columbia   d. Rio Grand

41. ★★ As you cruise past New Orleans, what does your narrator tell you this city is rich in besides history, music, and good food?

a. Voodoo   c. Alligators

b. Ghost Stories   d. Bayou

42. ★★ Who does your narrator say can shed some light on the happenings on Splash Mountain?

a. Brer Fox   c. Brer Frog

b. Brer Bear   d. Brer Rabbit

43. ★★ As you hear the singing out of the depth of the river, what is the sweetest sound a river man can hear according to your narrator?

a. Mark One   c. Mark Three

b. Mark Two   d. Mark Twain

Did you know?

Along the right riverbank you will see a log cabin in the wilderness. When Disneyland first opened and through several decades, this cabin would appear to be on fire. But with the decades, the cabin was extinguished and now rests as a constant reminder of the brave pioneers that settled this great nation we call home.

44. ★ As you see the Indiana Chief on his horse, what does the hand sign he is making signify?

a. Peace   c. Friendship

b. War   d. Hospitality

45. ★★ As you reach the Indian camp, which tribe are these Native Americans?

a. Hopi   c. Cherokee

b. Plains   d. Navajo

46. ★★ As you pass by, which Indian is passing on knowledge to the braves?

a. Chief   c. Shaman

b. Medicine Man   d. Warrior

47. ★★ As your narrator tells you to keep an eye out for wildlife, which of these is *not* one of the animals he mentions?

a. Moose   c. Mountain lion

b. Eagle   d. Beaver

48. ★★ As you continue your cruise on the Mark Twain Riverboat, what does your narrator tell you Tom Sawyer has always wanted to be?

a. A captain   c. A pirate

b. A cowboy   d. A runaway

Bonus Question

49. ★★★ As you round the back side of Tom Sawyer Island, what song is playing on the Mark Twain riverboat?

a. Red River Valley

b. Old MacDonald

c. My Old Kentucky Home

d. Davy Crockett

Did you know?

As you look at the left bank just before you arrive back at the dock, you will see several artifacts from the long-retired Rainbow Ridge attractions from the origins of Disneyland.

Big Thunder Mountain Railroad

50. ★ As you approach Big Thunder Mountain Railroad, you will find the city sign for Rainbow Ridge. What was the original population of this western town?

a. 38   c. 2015
b. 247   d. 1502

51. ★ As you enter the queue for Big Thunder Mountain
     Railroad, what is the date you see on the Big Thunder
     Mine Chute?

     a. 1980   c. 1680
     b. 1870   d. 1880

52. ★ As you continue your trail to Big Thunder Mountain
     Railroad, you will find some supplies near the walkway,
     what does the label for the blasting powder read?

     a. Dumbo   c. Jumbo
     b. Jimbo   d. Limbo

53. ★★ As you walk past the town of Rainbow ridge to your
     right, in what year did the Assay office establish?

     a. 1869   c. 1955
     b. 1969   d. 1855

54. ★★★ As you look at the door of the hotel, what does the
     writing advertise?

     a. Vacancy   c. Softest beds in town
     b. Best food in town   d. Best prices in town

55. ★★ At the end of Rainbow Ridge, you will find the
     Mercantile. If you read the chalk board out front, how
     much are the boots?

     a. $10   c. $100
     b. $50   d. $20

56. ★★ As you look at the front of the Mercantile, how
     much is a cigar?

     a. 25 cents   c. $10
     b. 10 cents   d. $2

57. ★★ If you look carefully at the tunnel next to the Mercantile, what is the name of the blacksmith on the sign above the tracks?

   a. Davy Crockett   c. Jeremiah Disney
   b. Mark Twain   d. Jeremiah Colt

58. ★ As you enter your ride train, listen to the safety warning. According to your narrator, this is the wildest ride in the _____.

   a. Wilderness   c. Town
   b. West   d. Plains

Did you know?

As you climb the first incline of your ride you will see water streaming from both sides. The rock formation in the center resembles Sleeping Beauty's castle.

59. ★ As you climb the second incline on your ride, you will see a ram at the top. What is he chewing on as you pass?

   a. Grass   c. Tin Can
   b. Dynamite   d. Flower

60. ★★ Across from Big Thunder Mountain Railroad, you will find a shipping office by the rivers of America. On the side of the building, you will find a mural. Which famous Disney character is seen on the deck of the Mark Twain Riverboat in this mural?

   a. Donald Duck
   b. Captain Jack Sparrow

c. Goofy

d. Mickey Mouse

Did you know?

As you follow the path towards Big Thunder Ranch, you will cross a small bridge. Look to your left and watch the water. Periodically, you will see a fish jump out of the water. Also notice across from the bridge a large tunnel. These are the last remnants of one of the original Disneyland attractions, the Rainbow Ridge Pack Mules.

Looking for hints on your way? Click here to find what you seek.

Tomorrowland

As you enter Tomorrowland from the Hub of Disneyland, you will experience space flight, interstellar bad guys, and some of your favorite super-heroes. Try your skill at Buzz Lightyear Astro Blasters or zoom through the stars on Space Mountain.

Having difficulty on your scavenger hunt? Click the link at the bottom of the chapter for hints to help you on your way.

1. ★ As you enter Tomorrowland from the Hub of Disneyland, you will find a plaque with the opening day speech Walt Disney gave on July 17, 1955. Finish

this line from that speech, "A step into the future, with predictions of _____ things to come..."

a. Destructive   c. Interesting

b. Fabulous   d. Constructive

Did you know?

If you look around at the plants within Tomorrowland you will notice they are all edible. From peppers to lettuce, agriculture is key to the future of our planet.

---

2. ★ As you walk toward the Astro Orbitor attraction, how many rocket jets do you see?

a. 12   c. 8

b. 10   d. 15

Buzz Lightyear Astro Blasters

3. ★★ As you enter the queue for the Buzz Lightyear Astro Blasters, look at the large walkie talkie just inside the doorway. What do the aliens say is the status?

a. Critical Mass   c. Bad, Very Bad

b. Status Quo   d. Good, Very Good

4. ★ As you look at the black and white operating instruction posters, what is the score total shown at the bottom?

a. 112146

b. 112164

c. 114126

d. 116124

> **Did you know?**
> As you look at the large picture of the galaxy with the various sections, look at the planet earth. One continent shows a profile of Mickey Mouse if you look closely.

5. ★ On the map of the galaxy, on which section is the planet Glinbaka located?

   a. 4   c. 6

   b. 5   d. 3

6. ★ In which quadrant is Star Command located, according to the map of the galaxy?

   a. Delta   c. Gamma

   b. Omega   d. Alpha

7. ★ As you see the famous Buzz Lightyear, what classic toy is used to draw the pictures he refers to?

   a. Etch A Sketch   c. Spirograph

   b. Light Bright   d. Leap Pad

8. ★★ As you walk past Buzz Lightyear and begin moving up the ramp, look at the alien game. What is the score on the console?

   a. 2046   c. 20465

   b. 20460   d. 20464

9. ★ Looking at the picture of the different targets, which color is the triangle target?

   a. Green   c. Blue

   b. Purple   d. Orange

10. ★★ As you enter your ride vehicle and begin your journey, what childhood toy floats next to the Boxobot?

a. Jacks   c. Blocks

b. Hula Hoop   d. Slinky

11. ★★ As you continue your ride through space, what side of the red die is facing you?

a. 1   c. 6

b. 5   d. 3

12. ★ As you begin your adventure, what does the read-out say on the Gigantobot?

a. Buzz Rules   c. Zurg Rules

b. Space Rules   d. Blaster Party

13. ★ As you pass between the first room and Zurg, how many electrical cords are plugged in above your head?

a. 3   c. 7

b. 5   d. 10

14. ★★★ As you pass by Zurg, finish the line he says to you, "Resistance is _____."

a. Pointless   c. Lasting

b. Futile   d. Deadly

15. ★ As you pass through the Planet Z surface, which of these is *not* one of the colors of the aliens hooked together?

a. Red   c. Yellow

b. Orange   d. Blue

Did you know?

As you pass through the darkened tunnel into the last room on your adventure, there are three hidden targets, two in the ceiling and one to your left.

16. ★★ As your space adventure comes to an end you will find two aliens with a receipt for Zurg. What is the price for Zurg according to the receipt?

a. $8.99   c. $12.99

b. $10.99   d. $14.99

17. ★★★ As you see Zurg in the package, what is the bar code number on the box?

a. 2080 6667   c. 2070 7776

b. 2700 7776   d. 7776 2000

18. ★ According to the ranking status board, which level is colored green?

a. Planetary Pilot   c. Galactic Hero

b. Space Scout   d. Star Cadet

19. ★ According to the ranking status board, which of these is the highest ranking?

a. Galactic Hero   c. Ranger 1st Class

b. Cosmic Commando   d. Star Cadet

• • • • • • • • • • • • • • •

20. ★ As you exit the Buzz Lightyear Astro Blaster, enter the Little Green Men Shop. Look at the mural behind the cash register area. What award was presented to Buzz Lightyear?

a. Golden Planet   c. Golden Alien

b. Golden Zurg   d. Golden Claw

21. ★ As you look at the pictures of Buzz Lightyear, what creature is the mayor awarding Buzz?

a. Lobster   c. Crab

b. Octopus   d. Whale

22.   ★★ According to the scroll to your left of the cash register counter, what award did the universe protection unit award to buzz?

    a.   Employee of the Month

    b.   Employee of the Millennium

    c.   Employee of the Decade

    d.   Employee of the Century

23.   ★ As you see the mural of the aliens present Buzz Lightyear with another medal, what does the writing above his head read?

    a.   Galactic Scout   c.   Our Hero

    b.   Congratulations   d.   Galactic Hero

Star Tours

24.   ★★ As you enter the queue for Star Tours, look up at the control room above you. Which classic Star Wars character is inside this control room?

    a.   Admiral Ackbar   c.   Boba Fett

    b.   Chewbacca   d.   Jabba the Hutt

25.   ★★★ As you listen to C3PO, what does he have no intention of getting another case of?

    a.   Rust

    b.   Oil Sludge

    c.   Dust Contamination

    d.   Bolt Rot

26.   ★★ As you observe the Star Speeder 1000, what is the code beneath R2D2's copilot?

    a.   IB360   c.   C3P20

    b.   IC360   d.   R2D3

27.   ★★ As you watch the boarding schedule on the screen, what is the status for flight 610 to Kashyyyk?
a.   On Time
c.   Gate Changed
b.   Delayed
d.   Cancelled

28.   ★★ As you watch the boarding schedule, what is the status for flight 104 to Ithor?
a.   Delayed
c.   Cancelled
b.   On Time
d.   Landed

29.   ★★ According to the boarding schedule, where does flight 1119 go to?
a.   Hoth
c.   Geonsis
b.   Naboo
d.   Kashyyyk

30.   ★★ As you watch the weather pass on the screen, what is the weather prediction for Coral City?
a.   Sunny
c.   Cloudy
b.   Scattered Showers
d.   Partly Cloudy

31.   ★ As you continue through the Star Tours station, read the direction sign. Which level is the Lightspeeder Lounge located on?
a.   4
c.   2
b.   5
d.   1

32.   ★★ According to the passenger services sign, what else is picked up with baggage claim?
a.   Land Speeders
c.   Droids
b.   Jawas
d.   Hovercraft

33.   ★★★ As you walk through the baggage area, notice the container for Droids. Which of these is *not* one of the requirements before shipping?

a. Power it down   c. Drain all fluids

b. Pack in Styrofoam   d. Backup all data

34. ★★ As you exit the Star Tours attraction you will enter the Star Trader shop. Above you are several containers marked for shipping. One is marked for shipment to the "Imperial _____."

a. Moon   c. Garrison

b. Palace   d. Temple

Did you know?

As you enter the Star Trader shop, look up at the ceiling. A scale model of an X-Wing fighter is suspended from the ceiling.

---

35. ★ As you exit the Star Trader store, look up at the marquee. How many neon astronaut Mickey's adorn the outside of this building?

a. 9   c. 6

b. 12   d. 8

Did you know?

Look across at the mural above the Buzz Lightyear Astro Blasters attraction. This mural covers an original mosaic by artist Mary Blair entitled *The Spirit of Creative Energies Among Children*.

Autopia

36. ★ As you begin your ride on Autopia, you will pass a billboard for food service. Finish this line, "You'll be _____ you did."

a. Thankful   c. Happy

b. Tankful   d. Fullfilled

37. ★ As you read the signs around you on the road, what is the route number you are traveling on?

a. 71   c. 55

b. 19   d. 81

38. ★ Look closely and you will see a sign with a Mickey head on it. What does this sign read?

a. Mouse Crossing   c. Character Crossing

b. Mickey Crossing   d. Minnie Crossing

Did you know?
As you exit the Autopia attraction you can get your own personalized drivers license with your picture. Check out the photo booths to get your souvenir!

Finding Nemo Submarine Voyage

Did you know?
When this attraction first opened, there were young girls dressed as mermaids in the middle of the lagoon. This stopped after several ardent young men jumped into the water to swim out to the mermaids on the rocks.

39. ★★ As you enter the submarine for your voyage, how many fathoms does your captain say to take her down?

a. 6   c. 12

b. 8   d. 10

40. ★★ As you see the lost city, which *Finding Nemo* character do you see diving?

    a. Darla   c. Gil

    b. Nigel   d. Dory

41. ★ According to your captain, what natural occurrence makes dramatic changes to the landscape?

    a. Earthquakes   c. Rain

    b. Volcano   d. Wind

42. ★ According to your captain, how long does it take the reef to grow one inch?

    a. 1 Month   c. 10 years

    b. 1 day   d. 1 year

43. ★ When you see Nemo with Squirt, where does Squirt tell Nemo to follow him to?

    a. Out to Sea   c. To the EAC

    b. To Squirt's Dad   d. To Nemo's dad

44. ★ When you are navigating the EAC, what does Squirt tell nemo to grab?

    a. His neck   c. Rock

    b. His dad   d. Shell

45. ★★ While you are in the sunken boat Marlin tells Dory he's looking for his son. What does Dory call Nemo?

    a. Fabio   c. Bingo

    b. Chico   d. Nemo

46. ★ When you see Bruce and his shark friends, he warns you to be careful. What wouldn't you want to happen?

    a. Bombs to explode   c. Submarine to sink

    b. Balloons to pop   d. Crash into the ship

47. ★ As you continue your voyage, what do you see that is pink and bouncy?

a. Octopus
c. Jellyfish
b. Coral
d. Balloons

48. ★ When you arrive at the underwater volcano, what are Nemo's fishtank friends doing?

a. Running Away
c. Telling Jokes
b. Chanting
d. Floating in Baggies

49. ★★ When Nemo and Squirt are telling their friends about the adventures, what does the little octopus do?

a. Dance
c. Ink
b. Cry
d. Hide

50. ★★ When Squirt meets up with his dad, which of these is *not* one of the greetings they give?

a. Shell
c. Noggin
b. Fin
d. Dude

51. ★ How does your submarine come back to the surface after your adventures with Nemo?

a. Floating on jellyfish
b. Pushed by sharks
c. Caught in fisherman's net
d. Blown out whale blowhole

52. ★ As you reach the surface once again, what does the captain fear you will encounter besides a sea serpent?

a. Poseidon
c. Eels
b. Mermaids
d. Neptune

53. ★★ As you exit the Finding Nemo Submarine Voyage, walk around the lagoon and you will see a buoy in the

water with Seagulls perched on it. How many Seagulls do you see?

a. 2   c. 4

b. 3   d. 5

Did you know?

As you continue following the perimeter of the lagoon around, you will come to a dead end in the fence. Notice that this is the only place within Disneyland that three different fences converge to meet.

Looking for hints on your way? Click here to find what you seek.

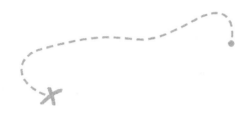

New Orleans Square

Wander the narrow streets and alleys of New Orleans Square, but be warned: you might have an encounter with pirates on your journey. Enjoy a mint julep while listening to some Dixieland jazz in this quaint area.

Having difficulty on your scavenger hunt? Click the link at the bottom of the chapter for hints to help you on your way.

Pirates of the Caribbean

> ### Did you know?
> One of the legendary rumors surrounding Pirates of the Caribbean is the story of Walt Disney's body being cryogenically frozen and placed beneath this attraction until a cure for cancer could be found. Walt Disney Passed away in 1966 and was cremated and placed with his family at Forest Lawn Glendale in a private ceremony. There is no validity to the rumor of his body being on Disneyland property.

1. ★ As you enter the queue for Pirates of the Caribbean, notice the plaque that commemorates this attraction. What anniversary was celebrated?

    a. 20th   c. 30th
    b. 50th   d. 25th

2. ★ Look carefully at the plaque before you, what date did the commemoration take place?

    a. March 17, 1997   c. July 17, 1997
    b. March 7, 1997   d. July 17, 2005

3. ★ As you enter the Pirates of the Caribbean building, notice the sign to your left. Finish the quote, "Dead Men _____."

    a. Abound   d. Travel with Davy
    b. Sail the Seas   Jones
    c. Tell No Tales

4. ★★ As you look around at the paintings in the queue, which of these is *not* one of the infamous pirates depicted?

    a. Captain Barbossa
    b. Captain Jack Sparrow

    c.   Sir Francis Verney

    d.   Captain Blackbeard

5.   ★★★ As you begin your journey, you will float through the New Orleans Bayou. As you see the old man sitting on his rocking chair in front of his shack, what song is playing?

    a.   "Oh! Susanna"

    b.   "Pirates Life for Me"

    c.   "This Masquerade"

    d.   "He's a Pirate"

6.   ★★ As you continue your cruise, what does the skeleton perched above your head say to get your attention?

    a.   Avast There!   c.   You down there!

    b.   Up Here!   d.   Belay there!

7.   ★★ As you listen to the skeleton's warnings, where does he say the plundering pirates lurk?

    a.   Around every bend

    b.   In every cove

    c.   At every turn

    d.   Where you least expect it

8.   ★ As you see the first pirate skeleton's lying on the beach, how many pirates do you see?

    a.   4   c.   3

    b.   5   d.   1

9.   ★ The pirate standing against the rocks has a creature resting on his hat. What creature do you see?

    a.   Parrot   c.   Dove

    b.   Raven   d.   Seagull

10. ★ As you enter the pirate tavern, what game do you see the two pirate skeletons engaged in?

   a. Darts   c. Shuffleboard
   b. Checkers   d. Chess

11. ★★ As you enter the pirate's sleeping chamber, what skeletal animal do you see with the pirate in the bed?

   a. Dog   c. Alligator
   b. Parrot   d. Shark

12. ★★ As you continue through the sleeping chamber, what instrument is playing in this room?

   a. Organ   c. Harpsichord
   b. Accordion   d. Violin

Did you know?

As you enter the treasure room, you will see a treasure chest on the far right side. This is the actual treasure chest prop used in the first *Pirates of the Caribbean* film.

13. ★★★ As you travel to the war between the pirate ship and the fortress, what is the name of the pirate ship?

   a. The Wicked Wench
   b. The Black Pearl
   c. The Flying Dutchman
   d. The Columbia

14. ★★ As you watch the scene with the villager being dunked in the well, what is the name of this man?

   a. Jose   c. Jack
   b. Carlos   d. Manuel

15. ★★ As you enter the buy-a-bride scene, what does the auctioneer call the men bidding?
    a. Bilge Rats   c. Fine Gentlemen
    b. Mateys   d. Pirate Swine

16. ★★ What is the auctioneer offered for the woman on the platform?
    a. Six pieces of gold
    b. Six bottles of rum
    c. Six keys to the treasure
    d. Six ship slaves

17. ★ How many Brides in total to do you see at the auction?
    a. 4   c. 6
    b. 5   d. 2

18. ★ How many pigs do you see in the mud with the sleeping pirate?
    a. 4   c. 2
    b. 5   d. 3

19. ★ As you see the pirate on the bridge above your boat, what color is the one stocking he is wearing?
    a. Red and blue   c. Red and white
    b. Black and white   d. Orange

20. ★ As you enter the jail cell scene, which of these is *not* one of the ways the pirates try to lure the dog with the key?
    a. A bone   c. A rope
    b. A dog biscuit   d. Whistling

21. ★★ As you see Captain Jack Sparrow sitting in the treasure room, what does he toast to?

a. Treasure c. Piracy

b. Captain Barbossa d. Scoundrels

22. ★★ As you enter the land above once more, what area does the treasure map to your right show?

a. Isla Tesoro c. Tortuga

b. Isla Nublar d. Port Royal

• • • • • • • • • • • • • • • •

Did you know?

As you wander New Orleans Square, look up at the area above the Pirates of the Caribbean entrance. This was to be used as a private apartment for the Disney family but was not completely before Walt Disney's death. You will notice the initials W.D. and R.D. for Roy and Walt Disney. This is now used as the Dream Suite of Disneyland resort.

23. ★★ As you walk up Royal Street, you will find an alcove with a pirate fortuneteller. What is the name of this pirate?

a. Jack Sparrow c. Fortune Red

b. Davy Jones d. Fortune Black

24. ★★★ As you look at the treasure map in the pirate's hand, which of these is *not* one of the directions to follow?

a. Ignore Lesser Treasure

b. Rest Stop

c. Step Over

d. Don't Be Misled

25. ★★★ As you wander through New Orleans Square, you will notice a veranda above the perfume shop. What does the tenant of this apartment do?

a. Play music   c. Knit

b. Sculpt   d. Paint

Did you know?

As you stand in the area of New Orleans Square near the restrooms, listen carefully. You will hear a voodoo woman talking from the veranda above.

---

26. ★ As you walk toward the New Orleans Square Railroad station, look around at the platform. How many large milk cans do you see?

    a. 3   c. 4

    b. 6   d. 9

27. ★ New Orleans Square reaches to the Rivers of America. As you head towards the river's edge, you will notice a large Anchor displayed. Whose ship is this anchor rumored to be from?

    a. John Lafitte   c. Blackbeard

    b. Jack Sparrow   d. John Lafoot

28. ★ According to the plaque on the anchor pedestal, what date was the battle of New Orleans?

    a. January 8, 1915   c. July 17, 1955

    b. January 15, 1908   d. January 8, 1815

29. ★★ As you continue walking by the River's of America toward the Haunted Mansion, you will notice a bricked archway. What is the year displayed above this arch?

    a. 1964   c. 1864

    b. 1764   d. 1674

The Haunted Mansion

30. ★ As you enter the queue for The Haunted Mansion, notice the antique funeral coach. According to the sign in the window, where can you apply?

   a. Guest Relations
   c. The Crypt Below
   b. City Hall
   d. Ghost Relations

31. ★★ As you walk past the pet cemetery, how many bird monuments to you see surrounding the cat monument?

   a. 5
   c. 6
   b. 4
   d. 10

32. ★★ On what date did Old Fly Bait die?

   a. August 9, 1969
   c. August 9, 1869
   b. July 17, 1969
   d. August 14, 1969

33. ★★ As you look at the pet cemetery, what is the name on the pig monument?

   a. Violet
   c. Rosie
   b. Petunia
   d. Napoleon

34. ★★ As you continue through the queue of Haunted Mansion, which of these is *not* one of the epitaphs on the crypts below the line?

   a. I.L. Beback
   c. M.T. Tomb
   b. Seymour Butts
   d. Rustin Peace

Bonus Question

35. ★★★ How many cemeteries are there in total in Disneyland? Bonus points if you can name them all. Check the answer key for the complete list.

   a. 5
   c. 9
   b. 6
   d. 7

Did you know?

The haunted mansion issued "I survived" certificates, at one time, to guests who requested them. The rumor of *death* certificates being issued has been circulating the Internet and magazine articles but has never been a fact. There are no death certificates available on this attraction.

36. ★ As you enter the Haunted Mansion, your ghost host says the ghosts practice their terror with what?

   a. Devilish delight
   b. Eerie delight
   c. Ghastly delight
   d. Ghoulish delight

37. ★ As you enter the stretching portraits, what does the label on the dynamite say?

   a. Danger
   b. Warning
   c. No Flame
   d. Kaboom

38. ★ What is the name on the epitaph of the grave the woman is sitting on?

   a. Thomas
   b. George
   c. Walter
   d. Ronald

39. ★★ As you enter the portrait hallway, what does the woman posed on the couch hold in her left hand?

   a. A fan
   b. A glove
   c. A bone
   d. A skull

40. ★★ As you continue along this corridor, what form does the woman in the final portrait turn to?

   a. Athena
   b. Medusa
   c. Belle
   d. Frankenstein's Bride

41.   ★★★ As you enter your doombuggy and begin your tour of the Mansion, which famous animated character is seen in the embroidery in the back of the chair next to the endless hallway?

a. Mickey Mouse   c. Pluto

b. Goofy   d. Donald Duck

42.   ★ As you pass by the casket in the parlor, what sits atop the casket?

a. Candlesticks   c. A raven

b. Wreath   d. One rose

43.   ★★★ As you enter the séance room, finish the line Madam Leota recites. "Wizards and witches, wherever you dwell, give us a hint, by _____"?

a. Casting a spell   c. Ringing a bell

b. Falling down a well   d. Singing right well

44.   ★★★ As you enter the dining room, how many candles do you see on the birthday cake?

a. 10   c. 14

b. 13   d. 15

45.   ★★ As you watch the dancers in the ballroom, how many couples do you see?

a. 4   c. 5

b. 6   d. 3

46.   ★★ As you enter the attic where the bride resides, how many times has she been married according to the wedding photos?

a. 5   c. 3

b. 6   d. 8

47. ★★★ As you see the bride, what is the year on the wedding photo beside her?
   a. 1955   c. 1877
   b. 1971   d. 1785

48. ★★★ What is the name of the bride's husband according to the wedding photo beside her?
   a. Reginald   c. Harold
   b. Arthur   d. George

49. ★★ As you enter the graveyard scene, you will see the ghost band playing, which of these is *not* one of the instruments being played?
   a. Bagpipes   c. Xylophone
   b. Lyre   d. Guitar

50. ★ As you approach the singing busts, how many of these statues have bowties?
   a. 4   c. 6
   b. 3   d. 5

51. ★★ As you continue your tour of the graveyard, how many ghosts did you see pop up from behind the graves?
   a. 6   c. 4
   b. 5   d. 8

52. ★★★ As you exit the graveyard, look up at the raven above. How many times have you seen the raven throughout the Haunted Mansion?
   a. 4   c. 7
   b. 5   d. 10

53. ★ As you enter the crypt, you will see the famous hitchhiking ghosts. What does the smallest ghost hold in his hand?

a.   Suitcase   c.   Hat

b.   Trowel   d.   Ball and chain

54.   ★ As you exit the Haunted Mansion, you see the small bride to your right. Finish her speech, "Hurry back, Hurry back. Be sure to bring your _____."

a.   Burial arrangements

b.   Death certificate

c.   Otherworldly possessions

d.   Loved ones

Did you know?

As you exit the turnstile of the Haunted Mansion, listen closely. You will hear the ominous laugh of the ghosts as you exit this building.

55.   ★ As you walk toward the rivers of America, you will see The Harbor Galley, Dockside Dining. According to the sign, who is the proprietor of this establishment?

a.   Walt Disney   c.   Jonathon Winship

b.   Widow Winship   d.   Master Gracey

56.   ★★ As you look beneath the sign, you will see a seaman with a yellow slicker. How many buttons do you see on the captain's coat?

a.   8   c.   4

b.   6   d.   10

Looking for hints on your way? Click here to find what you seek.

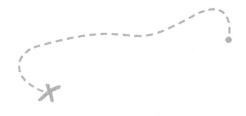

Critter Country

Join your favorite animal friends from your favorite classic Disney films in this rustic area of Disneyland.

1. ★ As you enter the Critter Country area of Disneyland, you will see a carved wooden sign greeting you. Which animal does the Fox stand on to balance the sign?
   a. Rabbit   c. Bear
   b. Squirrel   d. Turtle

2. ★ As you come into this area, you will see the canoe attraction to your right. Which famous explorer does this attraction take its name from?

a. Pocahontas   c. Lewis and Clark

b. Davy Crockett   d. Sacagawea

3. ★★★ As you continue into Critter Country, you will see The Hungry Bear restaurant. As you enter the lower level, you will find the restrooms. Which famous country bear adorns the sign outside the men's room?

a. Big Al   c. Liver Lips

b. Gomer   d. Henry

4. ★ As you stand at the entrance to The Hungry Bear restaurant, what does the waiter bear hold on his tray?

a. Ham sandwich   c. Fish and chips

b. Fried chicken   d. Hamburger

5. ★ As you look across from The Hungry Bear, you will find The Briar Patch shop. As you enter, look up at the ceiling. What vegetable is poking through the ceiling?

a. Carrots   c. Potatoes

b. Radishes   d. Beets

6. ★★ Above the mantle of the fireplace is a carved portrait. Which famous Disney character is the subject of this portrait?

a. Brer Fox   c. Brer Bear

b. Brer Rabbit   d. Winnie the Pooh

The Many Adventures of Winnie the Pooh

7. ★ As you enter the attraction, what color is "Winnie the Pooh" on the sign above the entrance?

a. Red   c. Blue

b. Yellow   d. Green

8. ★★ As you begin your journey, in the Blustery Day scene, which character says "Happy Windsday"?

   a. Winnie the Pooh   c. Roo

   b. Kanga   d. Gopher

9. ★ In the flood scene, what object does Piglet stand on to be saved?

   a. Hunny pot   c. Tree branch

   b. Chair   d. Bed post

10. ★ In the flood scene, which character is upside down in a hunny pot?

    a. Winnie the Pooh   c. Kanga

    b. Rabbit   d. Tigger

11. ★ In the dream scene, where did Winnie the Pooh fall asleep?

    a. In bed   c. Under the window

    b. At the kitchen table   d. In his easy chair

12. ★ In the Heffalump scene, what colors are the watering cans that are putting out the candle?

    a. Red and yellow   c. Black and white

    b. Blue and green   d. Red and blue

Did you know?

As you exit this room look directly above you as you enter the next room. The three animal heads from The Country Bear Jamboree sit in silence. This is a nod to the original attraction that occupied this space.

---

13. ★ As you see Winnie the Pooh stuck in the hunny, what does he say?

a. Help me

b. What a horrible dream

c. I am very full

d. What a wonderful dream

14. ★ As you enter Winnie the Pooh's house, what are the characters celebrating?

a. Christmas

b. Thanksgiving

c. Pooh's birthday

d. Christopher Robin's birthday

15. ★★ At the party scene, how many balloons hover above the table?

a. 8   c. 10

b. 6   d. 4

16. ★★ As you begin your exit from this attraction, look closely at the gifts from Pooh's friends. What is the title of the book from Owl?

a. Honey Discomfort   c. Honey and Me

b. 1,000 uses for Honey   d. Honey Remedies

17. ★★ How many Carrots has Rabbit put in the honey pot for Pooh?

a. 5   c. 8

b. 4   d. 1

18. ★★ As you look at the balloons on the last presents, which characters picture adorns the green balloon?

a. Rabbit   c. Christopher Robin

b. Owl   d. Winnie the Pooh

Splash Mountain

19. ★ As you begin making your way to the entrance of Splash Mountain, you will notice a door to your left marked "cast members only." What does the sign on this door say is inside?
    a. Cane Sugar
    c. Tree Sap
    b. Maple Syrup
    d. Molasses Vats

20. ★ As you enter the barn entrance for Splash Mountain, look around at the items scattered around the barn. How many clothes pins do you see in the metal bucket?
    a. 5
    c. 7
    b. 6
    d. 8

21. ★ Read the story signs around you as you walk through the queue. Finish this phrase. "Now this tale didn't happen just _____, nor the day before...."
    a. Recently
    c. Today
    b. Yesterday
    d. The other day

22. ★ As you pass by the statue of Brer Fox, Brer Bear and Brer Rabbit, what does Brer Fox hold in his hand?
    a. Axe
    c. Saw
    b. Hammer
    d. Club

23. ★ Read the story signs around you after you climb the stairs. Finish this phrase, "This tale happened once upon a time, not your time, not yet _____... but one time."
    a. His time
    c. Her time
    b. My time
    d. Their time

24. ★ According to the warning sign you will see, how many feet is the plunge ahead?

a. 40 feet   c. 50 Feet

b. 50 Yards   d. 40 Yards

25. ★★ As you enter your log and begin your journey on Splash Mountain you will find some antique items to your right. What name is printed on the large red press?

a. Chattanooga   c. Chatting

b. Chatterley   d. Charity

26. ★★ As you make your way around the briar patch and into the storage shed, according to the board, how many jars of molasses do they need?

a. 22   c. 12

b. 55   d. 14

27. ★★ As you pass by the houses for the animals, which of these is *not* one of the houses you see?

a. Brer Fox   c. Brer Bear

b. Brer Rabbit d. Brer Skunk

28. ★ You will find several containers of fruits and vegetables to your right, which of these fruits will you find in the wheel barrow?

a. Pumpkins   c. Watermelons

b. Carrots   d. Cantaloupe

29. ★ As you enter Splash Mountain you will find several birds to your right with a snowman. What is this snowman made from?

a. Snow   c. Watermelons

b. Pumpkins   d. Tumbleweeds

30. ★★ Next you will find a sleeping alligator. What creature is sleeping on his back?

a. Bunny　　　　　c. Frog

b. Bird　　　　　　d. Alligator

31. ★ As you float along you will find Brer Rabbit with one of his friends to your right. What creature is he standing with?

a. Alligator　　　　c. Bear

b. Fox　　　　　　d. Turtle

32. ★★ You will notice Brer Rabbit above your head further down the path. What is he riding on?

a. Handcart　　　　c. Wagon

b. Bicycle　　　　　d. Sled

33. ★★ According to the warning sign you see to your left, what is *not* allowed?

a. Frowns　　　　　c. Laughter

b. Screams　　　　　d. Smiles

34. ★★ When you find Brer rabbit finally caught by Brer Fox, what is the rabbit stuck in?

a. Tar　　　　　　c. Quicksand

b. Honey　　　　　d. Mud

35. ★ As you pass by the rabbit family, how many bunnies is the mother rabbit feeding?

a. 3　　　　　　　c. 4

b. 5　　　　　　　d. 2

36. ★ As you begin your climb to the final drop, what type of birds warn you of what's ahead?

a. Bluebirds　　　　c. Vultures

b. Storks　　　　　d. Pigeons

37.   ★ After you survive your drop into the briar patch, you will enter the finale of Splash Mountain. According to the signpost, what is the name of this place?

a.   Splash Landing   c.   Doo Dah Bend

b.   Doo Dah Landing   d.   Splash Bend

38.   ★★ Take a look at the large paddle boat, what instrument is the male pig playing?

a.   Guitar   c.   Accordion

b.   Drums   d.   Organ

39.   ★★★ Look closely at the paddle boat. What is the name of the captain?

a.   Andy   c.   Walter

b.   Anthony   d.   Albert

40.   ★★ If you look closely to the left of the paddle boat, what creature do you find celebrating all by himself?

a.   Rabbit   c.   Bluebird

b.   Turtle   d.   Blackbird

41.   ★★ As you finish your ride on Splash Mountain you will walk toward the picture area. Take a look around. What does the label read on the box in front of the copper pot?

a.   Extra Lens Caps   c.   Camera Straps

b.   Burnt Bulbs   d.   Film

42.   ★★ You will find a cabinet covered in chicken wire on the wall in this area. What does the label on the clear jar read?

a.   Picture Perfect Film

b.   Picture Perfect Developer

c.   Fixative

d.   Dark Room Drinks

• • • • • • • • • • • • • • • •

43.   ★ As you exit this attraction you will find Pooh's Corner across the road. Whose house sits outside to the right of the entrance to this store?

a.   Mr. Sanders   c.   Mrs. Kanga

b.   Mr. Rabbit   d.   Mr. Bluebird

44.   ★★ As you enter the candy store in Pooh Corner, what event is being celebrated?

a.   Owl's birthday

b.   Christopher Robin's birthday

c.   Tigger's birthday

d.   Pooh's birthday

45.   ★ As you look around the room above your head, you will find a large contraption above the area where the candy makers are working. What is this machine labeled?

a.   Rabbit's Carrot Shredder

b.   Owl's Seed Stripper

c.   Pooh's Hunny Mixer

d.   Eeyore's Thistle Grower

46.   ★★ As you exit this store, look up at the building very carefully. What year was Critter Country established?

a.   1889   c.   1955

b.   1989   d.   2001

47.   ★ Outside the Pooh Corner shops, you will find the meet-and-greet area for Pooh and his friends. According to the signpost in this area, which area is written on the yellow sign?

a.   Rabbit's Garden   c.   Piglet's House

b.   Gopher's House   d.   Eeyore's House

48.   ★ As you walk around the meet-and-greet area you will find a stack of hunny pots, how many are stacked high?

    a.   5   c.   6

    b.   7   d.   8

49.   ★★ As you look at Rabbit's garden, how many carrots do you see?

    a.   13   c.   15

    b.   17   d.   10

50.   ★ According to the sign, who is required to stay out of Rabbit's garden?

    a.   Tigger   c.   Owl's

    b.   Eeyore's   d.   Goffer's

Looking for hints on your way? Click here to find what you seek.

As you finish your tour of Disneyland, prepare yourself for continued wonders at Disney's California Adventure park in part two of this book.

Disney's
California
Adventure

Introduction

Disney's California Adventure came to the Disneyland resort in 2001 showing the guests of the Disneyland resort the wonders of California all in one place. From the streets of Hollywood in the golden era to the boardwalks of Santa Monica, California Adventure has continued the tradition of wonder and excitement.

The resort excites guests with attractions like The Twilight Zone Tower of Terror and California Screamin' while continuing the tradition of family entertainment with Toy Story Mania and Monster's Inc. A brand new millennium of entertainment has blossomed at Disney's California Adventure theme park allowing new generations of guests to explore the themed areas with new enthusiasm.

Buena Vista Street

Welcome to Hollywood in the 1920's, the same decade Walt Disney and his brother arrived to make their fortunes. Buena Vista Street embodies the nostalgia of a time long past where you can visit the Five & Dime or shop and Mortimer's Market.

Having difficulty on your scavenger hunt? Click the link at the bottom of the chapter for hints to help you on your way.

Oswald's Tires

1.   ★ As you enter Disney's California Adventure you will encounter Oswald's Tire shop. You will see a car waiting for service, what is the make of this car?

a. Packard   c. Chevrolet

b. Ford   d. Rolls Royce

2.   ★★ As you enter Oswald's, you will see two license plates above the cash register area. What is the date on these license plates?

a. 1955   c. 1935

b. 1971   d. 1901

3.   ★★ As you look around Oswald's, you will notice a time table for the Pacific Electric. What is the date on this time table?

a. July 17, 1955   c. December 1, 1955

b. December 1, 1922   d. July 17, 1922

4.   ★★★ Oswald's displays the first dollar earned in a frame on the wall. Which of these is the correct letter for the serial number for this bill?

a. U   c. S

b. V   d. W

5.   ★★ Outside at Oswald's you will find the air compressor. Which number does the needle point to?

a. 70   c. 20

b. 55   d. 30

6.   ★ As you stand near the City Chamber of Commerce at First Aid, find the advertisement for Elias & Company. How many days a week are they open?

a. 7   c. 5

b. 6   d. 2

7.   ★ As you continue your exploration of Buena Vista Street, you will find the flagpole with the dedication. What date was Disney's California Adventure dedicated?

   a.   July 17, 2001   c.   February 8, 2001
   b.   February 8, 2000   d.   July 27, 2000

8.   ★ According to the dedication, what above all continues to inspire?

   a.   People   c.   Stories
   b.   Dreamers   d.   Land

Mortimer's Market

9.   ★★ As you walk to Mortimer's market, notice the billboard above. What is the name of the train on this advertisement?

   a.   California Dreams
   b.   California Limited
   c.   California Unlimited
   d.   California Travel

10.   ★ As you enter the market, look around at the shelves and you will find a box of newspapers. What day of the week is displayed on these newspapers?

   a.   Tuesday   c.   Friday
   b.   Thursday   d.   Wednesday

11.   ★ As you continue your examination of the displays, find the cans stacked neatly with butterflies on the label. What product lies within these cans?

   a.   Salmon   c.   Cocoa
   b.   Milk   d.   Tomatoes

12.   ★ What item sits atop the canister of Armor's fresh cold pack fruit?

   a.   Wooden crate   c.   Radio
   b.   Banana's   d.   Oranges

13. ★★ Take a peek around the corner from the market toward the locker area, you will see the sign for the Elysian Arcade. Which of these is *not* one of the stores listed on the sign?
   a. Atwater Ink & Paint
   c. Big Top Toys
   b. Trolley Treats
   d. Julius Katz & Sons

Kingswell Camera Shop

14. ★★ Walk through the sliding doors into Kingswell Camera Shop. On the wall, you will see a framed photograph of Los Angeles with a trolley. What number is on the side of the trolley in this picture?
   a. 901
   c. 201
   b. 701
   d. 107

15. ★★★ As you look at the collage of satisfied customer pictures on the wall, how many pictures do you see?
   a. 64
   c. 80
   b. 74
   d. 90

Julius Katz & Sons

16. ★ As you exit the Julius Katz & Sons shop, take a look at the window display. What does the description on the television read?
   a. Newfangled Television
   b. Modern Television
   c. Latest Model Television
   d. Futuristic television

> **Did you know?**
> If you look very closely at the window display of Julius Katz &
> Sons, you will find a Haka Autoknips device. This is one of the first
> camera self-timers on the market, allowing amateur photographers
> to have time to get into their photographs.

17. ★★ Enter the Julius Katz & Sons shop and look at the shelves around this store. You will find several items waiting to be fixed on the shelves. What does the tag read on the broken rectangular lamp?

   a. Ugly
   c. Brand New
   b. Needs Blub
   d. Unfixable

18. ★★ What does the tag on the blue clock read?

   a. Blue Clock
   c. Battery Needed
   b. Blue? Really?
   d. Paint Red

19. ★★ Next to the clock with the tag reading "fix glass" you will find a blue teapot. What does the tag read?

   a. Coffee Only
   c. I'm a Little Teapot
   b. Iced Tea Only
   d. Short and Stout

20. ★ As you continue down this side of Buena Vista Street, you will find the Atwater Ink & Paint store. Look up at the hanging sign above you. How many paint brushes are seen on the Learn to Paint sign?

   a. 6
   c. 4
   b. 2
   d. 5

21. ★ As you stand in front of the Atwater Ink & Paint store, find the sign sharing the names of the art instructions for the School of Art and Animation. Which of these is *not* one of the names listed?

a. Kimball   c. Reitherman

b. Disney   d. Kahl

22. ★★ As you peer inside the window of Atwater Ink & Paint, you will see a poster with Mickey Mouse. How many strings are on the guitar Mickey is playing?

a. 2   c. 5

b. 3   d. 1

Trolley Treats

23. ★ As you continue down Buena Vista Street, what is the next stop, according to the candy store window?

a. Candy Land   c. Candy Mountain

b. Candy Palace   d. Candy Shop

24. ★★ As you peer inside the candy store window you will see several yellow signs for the various candies sold. Which of these is *not* one of these yellow signs?

a. Chocolate Kisses   c. Ribbon Candy

b. Caramel Chews   d. Red Hots

25. ★ As you enter Trolley Treats, seek out the antique candy machine. What price is displayed for the Nemo's Frolicking Frisk candies?

a. 10 Cents   c. 5 Cents

b. 25 Cents   d. One Dollar

26. ★ What kind of candy is contained in the O-Zell package?

a. Banana Bites   c. Taffy

b. Licorice   d. Jelly Beans

27. ★★ On the opposite side of Buena Vista Street towards the entrance to Disney's California Adventure you will

find a metal grate at the curb in front of the Five & Dime store. What symbol do you see on this grate?

a. Waves   c. Boat

b. Fish   d. Sun

Did you know?

If you look along the left side of Buena Vista Street you will find a small alcove with a short set of stairs. At the top of these stairs is a set of mailboxes. You will find one mailbox marked E Valiant depicting Eddie Valiant from *Who Framed Roger Rabbit*, as well as T. Ogelvie, a character from the classic *The Apple Dumpling Gang*.

Five & Dime

28. ★★ As you enter the Five & Dime store on Buena Vista street, you will find a display of sunglasses and house slippers on the shelves above you. According to the sign, how much is women's hosiery being sold for?

a. $1.00   c. $2.00

b. 25 Cents   d. $1.50

29. ★★ Continue your search of the shelves above you and you will find a display with an old-fashion typewriter. According to the advertisement for ink, how many bottles can you get for 10 cents?

a. 1

b. 2

c. 5

d. 3

Big Top Toys

30. ★ As you walk toward the back of Big Top Toy Store, you will find a large circus mural on the wall. How many lions can you find within this mural?

   a. 2   c. 3
   b. 5   d. 1

31. ★ As you examine the mural, find the young acrobat woman standing on horseback. What color dress is this circus performer wearing?

   a. Yellow   c. Blue
   b. Red   d. Green

32. ★ As you come to the hub of Disney's California Adventure, you will find a statue of Walt Disney and Mickey Mouse in bronze. What is the name of this statue?

   a. Storytellers   c. Partners
   b. Friends   d. Legends

33. ★ Read the dedication of this statue. What was Walt Disney's suitcase made from?

   a. Wood   c. Carpet
   b. Cardboard   d. Leather

34. ★★ As you examine the statue of Walt Disney and Mickey Mouse, what is the number of the luggage tag on Mickey's suitcase?

   a. 111282   c. 828111
   b. 112821   d. 111828

35. ★ What item is in the breast pocket of Walt Disney's coat resting over Walt's shoulder?

   a. Envelope   c. Pen
   b. Paintbrush   d. Keys

Carthay Circle Resturant

36. ★ As you stand in front of the Carthay Circle, what is written on the curb in front of this building?

a. Valet   c. No Dumping

b. Valley   d. No Parking

Did you know?

At the Carthay Circle restaurant, you can enjoy cocktails and snacks in the public lounge while immersing yourself in the décor and photos of Hollywood premieres.

Did you know?

In the display case in the lobby of Carthay Circle you will find artifacts from classic Disney movies. The Disney archives provide these items for the pleasure of the guests and the displays are updated regularly.

---

37. ★★★ As you approach the reservation desk you will see a large portrait on the wall. Who is the woman with Walt Disney in this photograph?

a. Julie Andrews   c. Lillian Disney

b. Diane Disney   d. Haley Mills

38. ★★ As you walk to the top of the stairs, you will see a portrait hanging on the wall to your right. What famous actress is seen in this picture with Walt Disney?

a. Elizabeth Taylor   c. Haley Mills

b. Shirley Temple   d. Annette Funicello

Did you know?

There are several private rooms that guests can reserve for private parties, from four to twenty people at a time.

Did you know?

You've heard about the private club at Disneyland, well California Adventure was not left behind. The 1901 club is another private area for guests to enjoy themselves just like Club 33.

Looking for hints on your way? Click here to find what you seek.

Grizzly Peak Airfield

Make you reservation at Grizzly Peak Airfield to soar above the clouds to see the wonders of California. When it's time for a rest, join your fellow sky jumpers for a burger or a cool drink.

Having difficulty on your scavenger hunt? Click the link at the bottom of the chapter for hints to help you on your way.

1. ★ As you enter Grizzly Peak Airfield, you will find a caution sign asking ground vehicles to give the right of way to what?

a. Personnel   c.   Buses

b. Aircraft   d.   Tow Trucks

2. ★★ As you walk toward the station wagon on your left, what outdoor sports equipment is tied to the roof of this vehicle?

    a. Raft   c. Canoe
    b. Tent   d. Row Boat

3. ★ As you examine this car, what are the first three letters of the license plate?

    a. Wed   c. Led
    b. Bed   d. Red

Humphrey's

4. ★★ As you read the notices next to Humphrey's, what movie is being shown at the Campfire Supper?

    a. *Snow White*
    b. *Nature's Half Acre*
    c. *Wildlife Adventures*
    d. *The Parent Trap*

5. ★ According to the notices on the bulletin board, where can you get a fishing license?

    a. Humphrey's   c. Roy's
    b. Walter's   d. Disney's

6. ★ Which nature group is meeting at sunset according to the notices?

    a. Hikers   c. Stargazers
    b. Mountain Climbers d. Bird Watchers

7. ★★ As you enter Humphrey's you will find post office boxes behind the counter. Which range of numbered boxes do you see?

a. 720-740   c. 740-865

b. 725-740   d. 825-840

8. ★ As you look at the signup sheets on the wall behind the counter, which of these is *not* one of the activities listed?

a. Nature Hikes   c. Bird Watching

b. Whittling   d. Rock Hounds

9. ★ As you exit Humphrey's, to the front of the store, which trail goes to the raccoon creek and the spotted bat caves?

a. No Man's Bluff   c. Eureka Lake

b. Dead Man's Bluff   d. Antelope Meadows

10. ★ As you examine the Condor Gas pumps, what is the price of a gallon of gas?

a. 36 cents   c. 75 cents

b. 25 cents   d. 26 cents

Smokejumpers Grill

Bonus Question

11. ★★★ Read the notices on the board across the road outside Smokejumpers Grill. What classic Disney movie does the Camp Inch reference come from?

a. *Pollyanna*

b. *Swiss Family Robinson*

c. *The Parent Trap*

d. *Old Yeller*

12. ★ As you enter Smokejumpers Grill you will notice three flags. What year were the Bearpaw Basin Smokejumpers established according to the flag?

a. 1955   c. 1971

b. 1957   d. 2001

13. ★ As you look around Smokejumpers Grill you will find a tank of fire retardant. What is the word in quotes on this tank?

a. Water   c. Mud

b. Dirt   d. Tar

14. ★ As you walk toward the condiment bar to your right, find the chalk board hanging on the wall. Where are the ferocious firefighters directed to apply?

a. Fire Station

b. Police Headquarters

c. Ranger Station

d. Ranger Headquarters

15. ★★ As you walk toward the back of the right side of the restaurant you will find a case with memorabilia. As you read the wooden medallion with the bear paw, what is the name of the club?

a. Little Growlers Club   c. Little Cave Bears

b. Little Bear Cubs   d. Little Bear Paws

16. ★★★ Now find the postcard to Millie pinned to the board. What recipe did Tricia try for her husband?

a. Grilled Chicken   c. Grilled Steak

b. Grilled Burgers   d. Grilled Pork Chops

17. ★ As you continue your tour of the objects on the walls, what musical instrument do you see above the windows?

a. Trumpet   c. Saxophone

b. Accordion   d. Clarinet

18. ★ As you walk to the opposite side of the restaurant you will find a warning sign above the side doorway. What activity does this sign warn against?

    a. Campfires
    c. Joy Riding
    b. Feeding the Animals
    d. Low Flying

19. ★ Toward the rear of the left side of this restaurant, you will find a large door. According to the sign, who besides the Heroes are proud to serve?

    a. Hotshots
    c. Champion
    b. Hercules
    d. Super Men

20. ★★ As you examine the shelves around you, find the three canisters on display. Which of these is *not* one of the labels shown?

    a. Tea
    c. Coffee
    b. Sugar
    d. Cream

21. ★ As you exit the restaurant you will find a large watch tower in front of the Soarin' Over California attraction. What is the name of the lookout station?

    a. Mt. Grizzly
    c. Mt. Muir
    b. Mt. Condor
    d. Mt. Sinai

22. ★★ As you look around this area, find the Preserve and Protect box. Within this box is a hand-written card signed by whom?

    a. Walt Disney
    c. Smokey the Bear
    b. John Muir
    d. Mark Sumner

23. ★ You will find several Smokey the Bear posters within this box. Which do you find in the lower right corner of the container?

a.   Story of the Forest

b.   Conservation Pledge

c.   Fire Prevention Week

d.   Save Your Forest

Soarin' Over California

24.   ★★★ Which famous actor gives your security checklist prior to your flight?

a.   Patrick Warburton   c.   David Spade

b.   Kurt Russell   d.   Josh Gad

25.   ★ As you are told to use the storage under your seat, what is the guest in the video wearing on his head?

a.   Goofy ears   c.   Mickey ears

b.   Sorcerer hat   d.   Princess hat

26.   ★★ What does your flight attendant refer to children as in the video?

a.   Little People   c.   Munchkins

b.   Children   d.   Little Aviators

27.   ★★ As your flight begins, which of these is your first destination?

a.   San Francisco   c.   Malibu

b.   Los Angeles   d.   Anaheim

28.   ★★ As you soar over the hot air balloons, how many do you see in the sky?

a.   5   c.   9

b.   3   d.   15

29.   ★ As you float past the waterfall, what recreational sport equipment do you see in front of you?

a. Hot air balloon   c. Parachute

b. Hang glider   d. Airplane

30. ★★ As you fly over the desert, how many jets fly past you?

a. 5   c. 2

b. 6   d. 7

31. ★ As you arrive at Disneyland resort in your flight. What time of year is represented?

a. Christmas   c. Easter

b. Halloween   d. Thanksgiving

Did you know?

As you watch the fireworks over Sleeping Beauty castle, keep a sharp eye and you will see a hidden Mickey briefly in the star bursts.

Looking for hints on your way? Click here to find what you seek.

Grizzly Peak

T he youngest of the Disney mountain range, Grizzly
Peak stands proud in this area of Disney's California
Adventure. Explore the natural wonders of California on
the trails of the Redwood Creek Trails or get soaked on Grizzly
River Run.

Having difficulty on your scavenger hunt? Click the link
at the bottom of the chapter for hints to help you on your way.

Grizzly River Run

1.   ★ As you walk from the airfield around towards Grizzly
Peak, you will find the Grizzly River Run attraction.
What does the large bear hold standing in front of this
attraction hold in his left hand?

a. Helmet
c. Canoe

b. Paddle
d. Lantern

2. ★ As you approach the loading queue, how many guests fit within each raft?

a. 8
c. 6

b. 10
d. 12

Grizzly Outfitters

3. ★ As you exit the Grizzly River Run attraction, next door is the Rushin' River Outfitters. Above the front window you will find a sign reading, "Let's Cut a Deal". What farming tool is this written on?

a. A saw
c. A shovel

b. An ax
d. A wheelbarrow

4. ★ As you read the signage outside the Rushin' River Outfitters, what do they offer to do to fish?

a. Fish Scaled
c. Fish Frozen

b. Fish Cleaned
d. Fish Shipped

5. ★ As you enter the Rushin' River Outfitters you will find a sign to your right, finish the line. "We love _____ with you."

a. To Bargain
c. Tea Baggin'

b. Toboggan
d. T-Shirting

6. ★★ As you walk to the rear of the store, you will find a painting of a man fishing. How many flies do you see attached to his hat?

a. 2
c. 4

b. 3
d. 5

7.   ★ As you find the Welcome to Bear Creek mural, what animal is featured on this mural?

a.   Eagle   c.   Beaver

b.   Bear   d.   Fox

8.   ★★ As you read the murals around the store, what is the elevation of Mt. Lassen?

a.   14,162   c.   13,157

b.   2001   d.   10,457

9.   ★ Among the memorabilia around the store is a dirt bike award. What is the object used for the award?

a.   Trophy   c.   Mining Pan

b.   Bicycle   d.   Pick-ax

10.   ★ What is the name of this dirt bike award?

a.   Dirt Demon   c.   Dirt Devil

b.   Bike Blaster   d.   Bike Bester

11.   ★★ As you browse the items around the bicycles, which of these is *not* one of the trails on the signpost?

a.   Spokebuster Trail   c.   Bent Wheel Pass

b.   Pedal to the Metal   d.   Zoom 'N Doom

12.   ★ As you come out of the store and back on the trail, you will find a wooden box atop a barrel. What can you purchase for five cents?

a.   Cold Shower   c.   Warm Bath

b.   Hot Shower   d.   Dip in the Stream

13.   ★★ As you continue your trail walk, find the bronze plaque for the Steam Donkey. Where did the steam engine first appear in California?

a.   Sacramento   c.   Eureka

b.   Gold Country   d.   Walnut Creek

Redwood Creek Challenge Trail

14. ★ As you approach the Redwood Creek Challenge Trail, you will find a collage of pictures of Russell and Doug. What does the sign in the center picture of Doug read?

    a. Wolf Wharf   c. Wolf Wall

    b. Snake Slide   d. Squirrel Scramble

15. ★★ As you enter the Trail and look at the map, a Post-it note from Russell tells you who he is looking for. What is the name on the note?

    a. Doug   c. Ellie

    b. Kevin   d. Mr. Fredrickson

16. ★ As you explore the trails to your left, you will come across a statue of a frog. What is the frog eating?

    a. Flies   c. The Moon

    b. Stars   d. A Bird

17. ★ As you continue your exploration, you will find the statue of Tol'-Le-Loo the mouse. What instrument does he play?

    a. Flute   c. Clarinet

    b. Violin   d. Drum

18. ★ As you read the signs about the various animals along the trail, how do the Tule Elk mark their territory?

    a. Leaving footprints

    b. Stripping bark

    c. Picking flowers

    d. Rubbing on the ground

19. ★ As you find the statue of Ah-Wahn-Dah the turtle, why does he sleep with one eye open?

a. To protect the moon

b. The watch his family

c. To protect himself

d. To protect the sun

20. ★★ As you find the Mt. Lassen Lookout Ranger Headquarters, walk inside. Which of these is *not* one of the pieces of forest ranger equipment found hanging on the wall?

a. Pail   c. Helmet

b. Shovel   d. Ax

21. ★ As you examine the map table, what does code 10-13 mean?

a. Talk Slower

b. Guest Present

c. Never mind-Bear Got it

d. Message Received

22. ★ As you read the key for the alphabet, what word is used for letter K?

a. Karate   c. Kermit

b. Kilo   d. Kite

Did you know?

As you work your way around the Wilderness trail, you will find prints of the various animals living in the wild. Find the wooden sign giving you the answer key and see how many prints you can identify

23. ★ As you come to the Millennium Tree, you will find the story of the Redwood trees. How long does it take for a new ring to grow?

    a. 10 Years   c. 1 Year

    b. 100 Years   d. A Lifetime

24. ★★ As you read the rings of this tree, what year did this tree begin to grow?

    a. 818   c. 1360

    b. 1178   d. 900

25. ★★ What event took place in 1360 according to the rings of this tree?

    a. Forest fire

    b. Indians paint rock art

    c. California is first mentioned

    d. Volcanic eruption

26. ★★ In what year did the gold rush begin at Sutter's Mill?

    a. 1812   c. 1781

    b. 1848   d. 1955

27. ★ As you read the sign for the Striped Skunk, from how far away can they spray an enemy?

    a. 10 Feet   c. 25 Feet

    b. 20 Feet   d. 15 Feet

28. ★ As you exit the Redwood Creek Challenge Trail and continue your exploration of Grizzly Peak, stop at the large water wheel to your left. According to the bronze plaque, how did the idea for this wheel come to pass?

    a. Pigs eating   c. Cows drinking

    b. Horses drinking   d. Sheep eating

Did you know?

As you continue following the trail around Grizzly Peak you will notice you have the choice of leaving the area or continuing the path around the back side of the Grizzly River Run attraction. Continue your tour with the following

29. ★ As you look off to your right, what does the warning sign near the hillside ask you to watch for?

    a. Rocks   c. Floods

    b. Animals   d. Bears

30. ★ You will find the Eureka Mine Shaft No. 2 on your travels. What does the storage sign on the double doors read?

    a. Cart storage   c. Ore storage

    b. Canoe storage   d. Raft storage

31. ★ The green route sign tells you to look for what on the path ahead?

    a. Bicycle   c. Trucks

    b. Hikers   d. Snowmobiles

Looking for hints on your way? Click here to find what you seek.

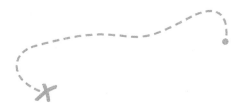

Hollywood

Transport yourself back to Hollywood in its hey-day as you spend time in this salute to glitz and glamour. Take a drawing class in the Animation Academy or take a ride on a haunted elevator. You may even see a celebrity or two on your way.

Having difficulty on your scavenger hunt? Click the link at the bottom of the chapter for hints to help you on your way.

1. ★★ As you enter Hollywood Street from Buena Vista Street, take a look at the signs around you. Which of these is *not* one of the signs in front of the Gone Hollywood store?

a. Fashion　　　　　　c. Accessories

b. Etcetera　　　　　　d. Menswear

2. ★ According to the sign at Award Weiner, finish this line: "Best Weiner in a _____ roll."

a. Supporting　　　　　c. Casting

b. Lead　　　　　　　　d. Genuine

3. ★★ At the corner you will find the Cahuenga Building. As you look in the window, what is the manufacturer of the typewriter you see on the desk?

a. Westwood　　　　　c. Underwood

b. Typewood　　　　　d. Overwood

4. ★★ As you peer in the window of the Cahuenga Building, what does the label on the film reels sitting in the floor read?

a. Pixar

b. Walt Disney Productions

c. Disney Brothers Cartoon Studio

d. Disney

5. ★★ As you look at the table with the cup, a film script for which animated feature sits below it?

a. *Pinocchio*　　　　　c. *Fantasia*

b. *Snow White*　　　　d. *Peter Pan*

6. ★ As you cross the street, toward the Off the Page building you will notice a parking meter at the curb. What is the status of this parking meter?

a. Violation　　　　　c. 30 Minutes

b. Time Expired　　　　d. Out of Order

Off the Page

7. ★★ As you look at the sign for Off the Page, which of these iconic characters is *not* on this sign?

    a. Timothy Mouse
    c. Mickey Mouse
    b. Minnie Mouse
    d. Lumiere

8. ★★ As you look at the ground in front of Off the Page, you will find a cell of Dumbo. According to the notes, what number does the animator refer to for the back of Dumbo?

    a. 69
    c. 79
    b. 763
    d. 190

9. ★★★ As you enter the Off the Page store, you will notice an artist table to your right with drawing papers surrounding it. Which of these characters from the film Snow White is *not* shown in these drawings?

    a. Snow White
    c. The Old Hag
    b. The Huntsman
    d. Dopey

10. ★ As you look above your head you will find several drawings coming to life off the drawing papers. Which character from *Peter Pan* is shown in full color coming off the drawing paper?

    a. Tick Tock Croc
    c. Mr. Smee
    b. Captain Hook
    d. Wendy Darling

11. ★ What color pencil is used on the drawing of Pinocchio as he is held by Geppetto?

    a. Red
    c. Green
    b. Blue
    d. Purple

12. ★★ As you search the tops of the cases around the store, what two characters from *Hercules* do you see lurking in the shadows?

    a. Hercules and Meg   c. Pain and Panic

    b. Hercules and Zeus   d. Hades and Meg

13. ★ As you find the drawing of baby Hercules and baby Pegasus, what color pencil was used to draw Pegasus?

    a. Red   c. Green

    b. Blue   d. Purple

14. ★★ As you search the tops of the cases around the store, what scene from *Cinderella* do you see above your head?

    a. Ballroom scene   c. Fairy godmother

    b. Sewing the dress   d. Getting married

15. ★ As you find the drawing of Ariel coming to life from the page, what does Sebastian appear to be doing?

    a. Pulling Ariel's Tail

    b. Conducting the Orchestra

    c. Running from a Shark

    d. Playing with Flounder

16. ★★ As you walk toward the back of this store you will find a doorway with a hallway beyond. As you exit through this doorway which movie is portrayed on the wall to your right?

    a. *Cinderella*   c. *Tarzan*

    b. *The Lion King*   d. *Mulan*

17. ★ Just above the doorway you just went through, what feathered character from *The Lion King* do you see?

    a. Simba   c. Zazu

    b. Scar   d. Nala

The Animation Studio

Did you know?

Guests can take drawing classes each hour to learn how to animate their favorite characters. Check the time-table to find out when you can draw your favorite character.

Did you know?

As you walk through the Animation Academy, a pathway that you to several secret rooms to animate cartoons. Enter the Beast's library to find out which Disney character you are and Ursula's grotto to play at voice-over work.

Schmoozies

18. ★ Across the street from the Animation Academy, you will find Schmoozies. What color is the outline of the lettering on the sign?

a. Blue   c. Red

b. Green   d. Orange

19. ★★ As you walk along the sidewalk next to Smoozies, you will find a wall with a mosaic made up of various unusual items. What color is the small piano you will find toward the left side of this mosaic?

a. Blue   c. Green

b. Pink   d. Black

20. ★★ Just below the fork in the Mosaic, what animal is embedded in the wall?

a. Dog   c. Dinosaur

b. Cat   d. Bird

21.　★★★ As you look around this mosaic on the right side of the building, how many spoons so you find?

a.　10　　　　　　　　　　c.　22

b.　8　　　　　　　　　　d.　14

22.　★★ In the red area of this mosaic on the right side of the building, what clear acrylic item is seen to the right?

a.　Building　　　　　　c.　Train

b.　Frog　　　　　　　　d.　Hat

23.　★★ As you look across the street to the left of the Animation Academy, which of these is *not* one of the shop marquees you see?

a.　Flowers　　　　　　c.　Pets

b.　Grocer　　　　　　　d.　Sweets

24.　★ Next door to the Fairfax market is the Argyle building. As you look in the window, you will see an old-fashioned type writer. What color is this item?

a.　Blue　　　　　　　c.　Green

b.　Red　　　　　　　　d.　Orange

25.　★★ As you look at the mail next to the typewriter, what is the permit number of the first class postage stamp?

a.　9735　　　　　　　c.　1971

b.　1955　　　　　　　d.　9375

26.　★★ As you read the brochure for European Travel Bargain, which of these is *not* one of the cities listed?

a.　Paris　　　　　　　c.　Glasgow

b.　Shannon　　　　　　d.　Berlin

27.　★ What price do you find from New York to six European countries, according to this brochure?

a. $453 c. $345

b. $543 d. $463

28. ★ Look carefully at the plane tickets on the desk. How many blue Pan Am tickets are fanned out together?

a. 3 c. 5

b. 4 d. 6

29. ★ As you continue walking through Hollywood, you will get to the corner and find the Hyperion Theater. As you look down the street, at what theater is the film *Fantasia* playing?

a. El Capitan c. Hyperion

b. Crest d. Grauman's Chinese

Monster's Inc. Mike and Sulley to the Rescue

30. ★ As you enter the queue for Monster's Inc. Mike and Sulley to the rescue, you will notice several posters to your right. According to the Monster News, they have won thirteen _____ awards.

a. Screamy c. Oozy

b. Emmy d. Drooly

31. ★★ As you look at the poster for Monster's Inc., what time does the center clock in the background read?

a. 8:45 c. 12:15

b. 10:27 d. 8:17

32. ★ As you enter the transit terminal, pause for a moment to read the monster passenger restrictions. Which type of monster is prohibited from sitting behind the driver?

a. Smelly c. Fire Belchers

b. Oversized d. Spiny

33. ★ According to the restrictions, you may not stick your tongue out the window if it is longer than ___ feet.
    a. 4   c. 7
    b. 5   d. 6

34. ★ As you finish reading the restriction sign, how many eyes does the drawn smiley face at the bottom of the page have?
    a. 5   c. 7
    b. 6   d. 2

35. ★★★ As you approach the phone booth, take a moment read the phone book below. What is the name of the optical business advertised?
    a. Cyclops   c. Iris
    b. Bug Eyed   d. Four Eyes

36. ★★★ According to the advertisement for the Monster City Café, which of these is *not* one of the offerings?
    a. Espresso   c. Cappuccino
    b. Latte   d. Diesel

37. ★ As you enter the queue for Monsters Inc. Mike and Sulley to the Rescue, you will notice a menu from Harry Hausen's on the wall. What is in the Terrible Teriyucki?
    a. Eels   c. Vulture
    b. Monsters   d. Bats

38. ★ Which of these is *not* one of the Sake offerings on the Harry Hausen's menu?
    a. Hot Sake   c. Flaming Sake
    b. Sake   d. Cold Sake

39. ★ As you continue through the terminal, you will find a newspaper machine. What is the name of the newspaper with the headline "Baby born with five heads"?
    a. *Glob*
    b. *Globe*
    c. *Blob*
    d. *Slob*

40. ★ As you find a vending machines close to the loading queue, which of these is the correct name of small snack bag?
    a. Bag O Carbs
    b. Bag O Snacks
    c. Bag O Calories
    d. Bag O Fat

41. ★ What does the print above Raccoon read on the box of snacks in the vending machine?
    a. Brand New
    b. New and Improved
    c. Old Dried Out
    d. Same Old

42. ★ According to the advertising signs across from the loading queue, how many foul flavors of monster mouthwash are there?
    a. 4
    b. 5
    c. 3
    d. 8

43. ★ What describes the flavors of Primordial Ooze according to the advertising?
    a. Super Tasty
    b. Super Natural
    c. Super Unnatural
    d. Super Duper

44. ★★ According to the Rabid Transit sign, which number will bring you to Monster's Inc.?
    a. 916
    b. 31
    c. 420
    d. 961

45. ★ As you begin your journey through Monstropolis, watch the television screen in your vehicle. What is the

number on the CDA workers suit that tells you they can neither confirm nor deny the presence of a human child?

a. 00001   c. 01955

b. 01845   d. 00002

46.   ★★ As you pass by Mike and Celia in Mike's car, what does he say to Celia?

a. Happy Birthday   c. I Love You

b. Merry Christmas   d. Close Your Eyes

47.   ★★ As you pass by the Grossery store, what does the first sign read on the fruit stand out in front?

a. Spooky fruit   c. Scream Fruit

b. Mangle Fruit   d. Crush Fruit

48.   ★★★ As you pass by the eye witness on the street, what happened to him after the child picked him up with its forked tongue?

a. He was thrown

b. He was tasted

c. He was rolled up and down like a yoyo

d. He was played with like a jump rope

49.   ★ As you first see Boo and Sulley, what is Boo's response when Sulley says, "Oh Boo, we gotta get you home."?

a. Kitty   c. Uh Oh

b. Mike Wazowski   d. Giggles

50.   ★★ What color is the phone the sushi chef octopus is holding to call the police in Harry Hausen's?

a. Blue   c. Green

b. Yellow   d. Black

51.   ★★ As you exit the restaurant, what does the CDA agent say they have in progress?

a. 2316   c. 2913

b. 2413   d. 2319

52.   ★★ As you enter Monster's Inc.; you will see two employees clock in for the night shift. What time is on the clock behind them?

a. 1:00   c. 2:00

b. 3:00   d. 8:00

53.   ★★★ As you enter the locker room where Mike and Sulley have Boo, which one of these items is *not* on the bench where Mike is standing?

a. Oderant   c. Contact Lens

b. Towel   d. Comb

54.   ★★ As you enter the scare floor where Randall is hiding Boo's door, how many days has the scare floor been accident-free according to the sign?

a. 52   c. 12

b. 47   d. 1

55.   ★ When you see Mike, Sulley, and Boo after Boo beats up Randall, finish this statement by Mike. "It's been the most _____ day of my life."

a. Terrifying   c. Terrific

b. Gruesome   d. Stressful

56.   ★ As you begin your exit of this attraction, how many eyes does the cameraman for the news station have?

a. 2   c. 3

b. 1   d. 4

> ### Did you know?
> As you approach Roz at the end of this attraction, she will interact with guest and choose people in the car to speak with or make personal comments.

Twilight Zone Tower of Terror

57. ★ As you enter the gates of the Tower of Terror attraction, in what year was the Hollywood Tower Hotel established according to the bronze plaque on the outside of the building?

    a. 1929   c. 1955
    b. 1921   d. 1919

58. ★★★ As you cross over the threshold into the lobby, look to your left. What card game do you see in process on the small table?

    a. Gin   c. Hearts
    b. Solitaire   d. Cribbage

59. ★★ On the table with the card game, you will find a hotel room key. What is the number on this key?

    a. 304   c. 403
    b. 221   d. 123

    Bonus Question

60. ★★ On the left couch, you will find a doll waiting for a young guest. What famous child star does this doll depict?

    a. Annette Funicello   c. Mary Pickford
    b. Shirley Temple   d. Darla Hood

61. ★★ What is the title of the book sitting on the couch next to the doll?

    a. *Alice in Wonderland*   c. *The Wizard of Oz*

    b. *Cinderella*   d. *The Little Mermaid*

62. ★★★ A gentleman guest has left his newspaper on the arm of a chair in the lobby. Finish this headline: "After six days, returns to asylum in _____."

    a. Hysterics   c. Pleasure

    b. Chains   d. Torment

63. ★★★ As you continue reading this newspaper, how was W.W. Milne found?

    a. Drowned in tub   c. Drowned in shower

    b. Drowned in pool   d. Drown in lake

64. ★★ In the chair closest to the fireplace, what type of craft item do you see resting on the chair arm?

    a. Knitting   c. Crocheting

    b. Needlepoint   d. Tatting

65. ★ On the arm of the couch you will find a magazine. What is the title on this publication?

    a. *Photoplay*   c. *Moviestar Weekly*

    b. *The Star*   d. *Screen Guide*

66. ★★ As you approach the registration desk of the Hollywood Tower Hotel, you will find a brass plaque describing the services. Which of these is *not* one of the services listed?

    a. Guest Registration   c. Room Service

    b. Cashier   d. Information

67. ★★ On the registration desk you will find several personal items left by a male guest. Which of these is *not* one of the items you see?

    a.   Handkerchief   c.   Coat

    b.   Hat   d.   Umbrella

68. ★ As you pass the registration desk, take a quick look behind the desk. You will find a newspaper waiting for a guest to pick it up. What is the name of this newspaper?

    a.   *Los Angeles Times*   c.   *Los Angeles Herald*

    b.   *Los Angeles Examiner*   d.   *Los Angeles Tribune*

69. ★★★ Behind the registration desk are mail boxes for the rooms of the Hollywood Tower Hotel. What number do you find in the upper right corner of these boxes?

    a.   1215   c.   1955

    b.   815   d.   1971

70. ★ As you cross over to the elevators in the lobby, you will find a directory. What lies on the top of the tower?

    a.   Lounge   c.   Tip Top Club

    b.   Sunset Room   d.   Steam Bath

71. ★★ As you read the directory, which of these is *not* on the lower level?

    a.   Gift Shop   c.   Beverly Room

    b.   Steam Bath   d.   Billiards

72. ★★ As you enter the library on your journey through the hotel, what game sits atop the table to your right?

    a.   Mahj ong   c.   Pai Gow

    b.   Dominoes   d.   Scrabble

73.　★★ As you examine the books on the shelves around the room, you will come across a set of books with green bindings. How many books are in this set?

a.　41　　　　　　　　　c.　36

b.　31　　　　　　　　　d.　39

Did you know?

If you look very closely at the volumes bound in green you will notice, all of the titles of the green books are names of *Twilight Zone* episodes.

74.　★★ If you count from right to left on these green volumes, what is the title of the sixth book you find?

a.　*What you Need*

b.　*The Most Unusual Camera*

c.　*The Lonely*

d.　*The Thing About Machines*

Did you know?

Within the book shelves are several volumes of guest books signed by all of the cast members who have had the privilege of working the Tower of Terror attraction. You may ask a cast member to point them out to you within the book shelves.

75.　★ Within the library you will find an ornate chair with several book volumes stacked on the seat. How many volumes do you find on this chair?

a.　8　　　　　　　　　c.　12

b.　5　　　　　　　　　d.　4

Did you know?

On the shelves above your head within the library you will find replica artifacts from the *Twilight Zone* television series.

76. ★★ As you exit the library and begin your adventure within the service area. Pause and read the bulletin board. Within the glass you will find a notice for play auditions. Read closely. What is the title of this play?

    a. *Romeo and Juliet*

    b. *Mid-summer Night's Dream*

    c. *Where is Everybody?*

    d. *What is this?*

77. ★★ According to the blue colored notice within this bulletin board, what event is coming up tonight?

    a. Costume Ball   c. Movie Night

    b. Dinner Dance   d. Retirement Dinner

78. ★★★ As you read the names on the time cards next to the time clock, what name is on the card in slot 10?

    a. Walt Disney   c. Franklin Gibbs

    b. Archie Beechcraft   d. Adam Grant

79. ★ Nearby on the wall stands a sign indicating the days without an accident. What is the number written in chalk on this board?

    a. 0   c. 31

    b. 13   d. 113

80. ★★ As you walk down this corridor you will find a boiler ahead of you. Look very closely at the side of this boiler. What does the read sign read?

    a.   Do Not Touch

    b.   Danger! Man in Boiler

    c.   Guests Prohibited in This Area

    d.   Enter at your Own Risk

81.   ★★ As you move through the loading queue for Tower of Terror and enter the elevator, what is the maximum load weight?

    a.   3 Tons   c.   300 Pounds

    b.   30 Tons   d.   3 Pounds

82.   ★ As you ride begins, your narrator tells you, "Wave Goodbye to _____."

    a.   Loved ones   c.   The real world

    b.   Universe   d.   Your sanity

Looking for hints on your way? Click here to find what you seek.

A Bug's Land

Shrink down to the size of a bug and enjoy the delights of the world around you. Find yourself in a giant garden or explore the underground with all your friends from *A Bugs Life*.

Having difficulty on your scavenger hunt? Click the link at the bottom of the chapter for hints to help you on your way.

1.　★ As you enter A Bug's Land you will see the A Bug's Land sign high above your head. According to the leaves hanging below, what kind of fun is for everyone?
   a.　Bug Sized
   b.　Pint Sized
   c.　Ant Sized
   d.　Fun Sized

2.   ★ As you enter A Bug's Land, you will see Flik the ant above your head to the right. What common object is he standing on?

    a.   Soda bottle   c.   Drinking straw

    b.   Corn cob   d.   Lamp post

It's Tough to be a Bug

3.   ★★ As you go below the ground to the It's Tough to be a Bug attraction, you will notice several posters for various shows. According to the poster for *Little Shop of Hoppers*, a grasshopper can jump how many times his own body length?

    a.   10 Times   c.   20 Times

    b.   5 Times   d.   100 Times

4.   ★ As you read the poster for *The Grass Menagerie*, what does the sign read that the bug holds up?

    a.   Help Me   c.   Surprise

    b.   Hello There   d.   Hi Mom

5.   ★ According to *The Grass Menagerie* poster, how many species of insects are there in the world?

    a.   8,000,000   c.   180,000

    b.   80,000   d.   800,000

6.   ★ If you read the poster for *My Fair Ladybug*, what are ladybugs?

    a.   Bugs   c.   Aphids

    b.   Beetles   d.   Insects

7.   ★ As you read the poster for *Antie*, Ants use their antenna to feel and what?

a. Taste   c. Smell

b. Talk   d. Hear

8. ★★ According to the poster for *A Cockroach Line*, Cockroaches are what kind of eaters?

a. Voracious   c. Constant

b. Picky   d. Vegetable

9. ★★ As you read the poster for *Web Side Story*, which type of spiders appear on the sign?

a. Black Widow   c. Daddy Long Legs

b. Tarantula   d. Wolf Spider

10. ★ As you read this poster for *Web Side Story*, how many times stronger is Black Widow venom than rattlesnake venom?

a. 10   c. 15

b. 20   d. 25

11. ★ Find the poster for *Barefoot in the Bark*. According to this poster, how high do the African termite mounds get?

a. 30 Feet   c. 50 Feet

b. 40 Feet   d. 45 Feet

12. ★ According to the poster for *Barefoot in the Bark*, how many termites can inhabit a single colony?

a. 2 Million   c. 4 Million

b. 3 Million   d. 5 Million

13. ★ As you read the poster for *Beauty and the Bees*, how many times a minute can bees beat their wings?

a. 26,000   c. 26,000,000

b. 36,000   d. 26

14. ★ According to the poster for *Beauty and the Bees*, how much honey is produced from 60,000 flowers?

a. One Quart   c. One Teaspoon
b. One Pint   d. One Cup

15. ★ As you take your seat in the theater and your show begins, the narrator requests you do not do perform certain activities. Which of these is *not* one of the items?

a. Jumping   c. Stinging
b. Pollinating   d. Chirping

16. ★★ According to Flik, how long have bugs been doing their act?

a. 30 million years   c. 3 million years
b. 300 million years   d. 300 years

17. ★★ As you watch the tarantula doing his act, what is his name?

a. Chewy   c. Chili
b. Changa   d. Willy

18. ★ What does the tarantula use for targets during his portion of the show?

a. Bugs   c. Seeds
b. Flowers   d. Acorns

19. ★ What famous tagline does the soldier termite use when he leaves the stage?

a. What you talkin' about?
b. I'll be back

c. Adrienne!

d. Yippee!

20. ★ What does Flik tell the stink bug to lay off?

a. Churros

c. Pretzels

b. Cotton Candy

d. Ice Cream

21. ★★ As Hopper takes over the show, he shows video of several bug films. Which of these is *not* one of the attacking insects?

a. Grasshoppers

c. Pill Bugs

b. Ants

d. Spider

22. ★ What is the name on the can of bug spray Hopper used to attack you in your seats?

a. Red Flag

c. The Bug Zapper

b. Bug Doom

d. Exterminator

23. ★ What food item does the bug show you at the finale of It's Tough to be a Bug?

a. Rotten cupcake

c. Rotten candy bar

b. Rotten churro

d. Rotten carrot

24. ★★ At the end of the show your narrator asks you to stay seated until the rest of the bugs exit the theater. Which of these is *not* one of the bugs mentioned?

a. Maggots

c. Cockroaches

b. Beetles

d. Grasshoppers

. . . .

25. ★★ As you exit and begin your exploration of A Bugs Land, you will walk through a large cardboard package. What is the name of this packing above you?

a. Buzz Lightyear Crunchies

b. Nemo Fish Crackers

    c.   Cowboy Crunchies

    d.   Mr. Potato Head Chips

26.   ★★ As you walk through the packaging you will find a picture of Sheriff Woody on the proof of purchase. How many tick marks appear on his sheriff star?

    a.   5   c.   1

    b.   6   d.   7

27.   ★ As you enter Flik's Fun Fair you will find a set of restrooms to your left. What common object does this building represent?

    a.   DVD box   c.   Popcorn bucket

    b.   Tissue box   d.   Candy box

28.   ★★ As you read the outside of the box making up the restroom building, finish this quote: "NEW, _____ to open box."

    a.   Sneezy   c.   Harder

    b.   Easy   d.   Impossible

Did you know?

As you explore Flik's Fun Fair, you will find a large garden hose with a sprinkler attachment in the center of the garden. You can play in the spray from this hose and cool off on hot days.

Flik's Flyers

29.   ★★ As you approach the Flik's Flyers attraction, notice the cartons making up the ride vehicles. Which of these is *not* one of the packages you find?

    a.   Chinese food box

    b.   Milk carton

c. Casey Junior cookies

d. Raisin box

30. ★★ As you read the carton for the cookie box, how many cookies does this box hold?

a. 20   c. 22

b. 12   d. 32

31. ★★★ As you read the Super Snack Pack box, what is inside?

a. Natural Peaches

b. Terrific Trail Mix

c. Homespun Applesauce

d. Old Fashioned Biscuits

Francis' Ladybug Boogie

32. ★ As you approach the Francis' Ladybug Boogie attraction, what common item holds up the wait time sign?

a. Drinking straw   c. Nut cracker

b. Sewing needle   d. Pencil

33. ★★ As you read the sign for Francis' Ladybug Boogie, what is the RPM for the vinyl record?

a. 33   c. 148

b. 128   d. 45

34. ★ How many ladybugs make up the ride vehicles of Francis' Ladybug Boogie?

a. 4   c. 10

b. 12   d. 6

Tuck and Roll's Drive 'Em Buggies

35. ★ As you enter the tent for Tuck and Roll's Drive 'Em Buggies, what is the trapeze bar made from above your head?

    a. Cotton swab   c. Sewing needle

    b. Toothpick   d. Safety pin

36. ★★ You will find the supports for the tent are made from drinking straws. Which of these colors is *not* one of the straws?

    a. Red   c. Yellow

    b. Blue   d. Purple

• • • • • • • • • • • • • •

37. ★★ As you wander around Flik's Fun Fair you will notice the benches scattered around. What objects make up the benches?

    a. Nail files   c. Popsicle sticks

    b. Rulers   d. Plastic spoons

Heimlich's Chew Chew Train

38. ★ As you approach the Heimlich's Chew Chew Train attraction, how many sprinkles do you count on the cupcake sign out in front?

    a. 32   c. 12

    b. 28   d. 128

39. ★ As you enter the train and begin your journey, what does Heimlich tell you he's looking for?

    a. His friends   c. Something to eat

    b. Health foods   d. The Circus

40. ★ Finish this line from Heimlich: "Carrots are orange, just like _____."
    a. Candy Corn   c. Lollypops
    b. Orange Slices   d. Gum Drops

41. ★ Heimlich must eat a lot of fruit if he wants to do what?
    a. Grow up big and strong
    b. Get longer
    c. Become a beautiful butterfly
    d. Grow a cocoon

42. ★★★ As your train goes through the watermelon tunnel, how many seeds are on the outside face of this fruit?
    a. 12   c. 21
    b. 15   d. 18

43. ★ As you pass by the package of Brussels sprouts, what kind of sauce does the package describe?
    a. Cheesy   c. Mushy
    b. Gooey   d. Runny

• • • • • • • • • • • • • • • •

44. ★ As you wander through Flik's Fun Fair, what common object are the garden lights scattered around?
    a. Pencils   c. Nails
    b. Pens   d. Paperclips

Looking for hints on your way? Click here to find what you seek.

Carsland

Walk down the street of Radiator Springs and relive the thrill of the movie Cars in real life. Meet your favorite reseidents, race for the Piston Cup or join Mater in a square dance.

Having difficulty on your scavenger hunt? Click the link at the bottom of the chapter for hints to help you on your way.

1.   ★★ As you approach the entrance to Carsland, you will see a large billboard. What Radiator Springs landmark is featured in the letter *A* in land?

    a.   Luigi's   c.   Mater's

    b.   Flo's   d.   City Hall

2.   ★ As you read the city limits signs of Radiator Springs, what is the elevation of the town?

    a.   159   c.   160

    b.   170   d.   165

3.   ★ Finish the sign that reads, "Association of _____ in the machine."

    a.   Cogs   c.   Screws

    b.   Nuts   d.   Wrenches

Taste-In

4.   ★★ As you get a cold drink from the Taste-In stand, what flavor of soda is housed in the blue drum with the orange writing in the top row?

    a.   Corn-fed Soy

    b.   Desert Yucca

    c.   Organic Raspberry

    d.   Free Range Seaweed

5.   ★★ What does the purple drum with the pink writing boast in the bottom row of drums?

    a.   Fermented   c.   High Desert

    b.   Steroid Free   d.   100% Whole

Mater's Junkyard Jamboree

6.   ★★ As you enter the queue for Mater's Junkyard Jamboree, you will find four license plates nailed to the post to your left. What is the county on the black license plate?

    a.   Rubberneck   c.   Parkway

    b.   Rollingstop   d.   Roadrage

7. ★ As you continue through the queue, stop for a moment to read the label on the bomb to your right. What's does Skipper's flight school guarantee?

   a. Parachutes that work

   b. Hardly any crashes

   c. We can teach anyone to jump

   d. We can teach anyone to fly

8. ★★ You will find the Mater moon rescue mission sign to your right. What is the name of the mission?

   a. Mustang XXX   c. Impala XIII

   b. Ferrari III   d. Wrangler VI

9. ★ According to the window you find in the queue, what is Mater's occupation?

   a. Farmer   c. Dentist

   b. Private Eye   d. Veterinarian

10. ★ The red white and blue signs scattered around read what about Mater?

   a. Great   c. Skater

   b. Greater   d. Awesome

Did you know?

As you exit Mater's Junkyard Jamboree, look for the petting zoo, where you can take your pictures with one of Mater's little tractors.

11. ★★ If you read the marquee for Tractor Feed and Farm Truck Association Hall, what day of the week do they meet?

   a. Wednesday   c. Saturday

   b. Thursday   d. Tuesday

Cozy Cone Motel

12. ★ As you arrive for your stay at the Cozy Cone Motel take a look at the various vendors. Which of these is *not* one of the vendors?

    a. Cone Coctions   c. Cone on the Cob
    b. Popcone   d. Churros

13. ★★ If you peek inside the registration for The Cozy Cone, you will find photos of national landmarks. Which landmark is seen in the oval picture frame?

    a. Stonehenge   c. Easter Island
    b. Eiffel Tower   d. Pyramids

14. ★★★ If you look at the registration desk, which Pixar character is found hiding beneath a road cone?

    a. Woody   c. Buzz
    b. Jessie   d. Slinky Dog

15. ★★★ How many cones total do you see on the shelves of the registration desk?

    a. 20   c. 18
    b. 30   d. 32

16. ★★ If you look closely at the cones on the bottom shelf behind the desk, what item are these cones made into?

    a. Radios   c. Carburetors
    b. Televisions   d. IPods

Radiator Springs Curios

17. ★★ As you continue down the street of Radiator Springs you will find Radiator Springs Curios. Which of these is *not* one of the gas pumps you will find outside?

a. Tulsa Tea   c. Butte Gas

b. Dinoco Gasoline   d. Oil Slick

Did you know?

When you enter Radiator Springs Curios, find the shelf above your head with the snow globes on it. The snow globe from the Pixar short *Knick Knack* appears on this shelf.

---

18. ★★★ If you find the Route 66 map within the Curios, it shows Route 66 beginning in California and ending in what state?

    a. Illinois   c. Missouri

    b. Arkansas   d. Kansas

19. ★★ Gaze around at the sticks on the shelves around you. What motor item does Lil' Torquey represent?

    a. Sparkplugs   c. Piston

    b. Brakes   d. Radiator

20. ★ Look above the doorway and you will find license plates lining the wall. Which of these is the blue California license number?

    a. 7BL28   c. W857142

    b. 332 959   d. 5B6748

Flo's V8 Café

21. ★ As you enter Flo's, notice the gas pumps around you. What price is the gas at these pumps?

    a. 53 cents   c. 73 cents

    b. 63 cents   d. 23 cents

22.   ★ On the windows of Flo's V8 Café you will read some of the offerings. Finish this sign "Fresh _____ Frosties."

a.   Frozen   c.   Frappe
b.   Frosty   d.   Freon

23.   ★★ As you enter Flo's V8 Café, find the red drink containers. What does the one with the yellow sign read?

a.   Yum   c.   Axle Grease
b.   Tulsa Tea   d.   Motor Oil

24.   ★★ Continue exploring Flo's V8 Café and you will find yourself in Doc Hudson's clinic. As you read the framed degrees on the walls, how many years did Doc Hudson attend the Internal Hydraulic Clinic?

a.   4   c.   2
b.   6   d.   7

25.   ★ According to the State Mechanical License, how long ago was this license issued?

a.   10 years
b.   2 weeks
c.   Many moons ago
d.   A long long time ago

26.   ★★★ As you find the X-ray of the engine, which citizen of Radiator Springs was X-rayed?

a.   Ramon   c.   Lightning McQueen
b.   Mater   d.   Luigi

27.   ★ As you check your eyes on the eye chart, what does line 8 read?

a.   ESREVER   c.   FDPLTCEO
b.   LOWGEARS   d.   DRIVE

28. ★★ As you examine the Healthy Combustion Chamber chart, what does number 4 on this chart represent?

    a.   Fuel Tank   c.   Fuel Line

    b.   Fuel Pump   d.   Fuel Line Inlet

29. ★★ At what number on the chart would you find the spark plugs?

    a.   4   c.   2

    b.   6   d.   14

30. ★ In what year did Doc Hudson receive his degree from Pnorthern Pneumatic Polytechnic?

    a.   1940   c.   1960

    b.   1950   d.   1955

31. ★ At what state did Doc Hudson receive his small business certificate?

    a.   California   c.   Kansas

    b.   Florida   d.   Confusion

32. ★★ Nearby, you will find several newspaper clippings of Doc Hudson's racing day. What is the tag line for *The Daily Exhaust*?

    a.   We Never Muffle the Truth

    b.   News that Wins the Race

    c.   Accelerating the Future

    d.   Driven by Passion for News

33. ★★ Read the newspaper with the headline "Hudson Hornet Winner 1951 Piston Cup". What is the name of the writer of the article to the left of Doc's picture in this paper?

    a.   Torque Wrench   c.   Knobby Tires

    b.   Fuel Combustion   d.   White Walls

34.   ★★ As you read the newspaper clipping with the headline, "Hudson Hornet champion for all time," how many years has this newspaper been running?

a.   82 years
c.   60 years

b.   94 years
d.   102 years

35.   ★★★ Behind the glass in the case. you will find Doc's Piston Cup prizes. How many wins did Doc have in 1952?

a.   37
c.   17

b.   12
d.   27

. . . .

36.   ★★ As you exit Flo's V8 Café and continue down the main street of Radiator Springs, you will come to the fire department. Which of these is *not* one of the departments in this building?

a.   Sheriff
c.   Drivers License

b.   Traffic Court
d.   Fire Department

37.   ★ As you stand before the Fire Department, what is the name of the founder of Radiator Spring?

a.   Mater
c.   Doc Hudson

b.   Stanley
d.   Mater Sr.

Did you know?

As you take a walk through Cars Land, take a look at the flower beds scattered along the road. The flowers are made from tail lights.

Radiator Springs Racers

38. ★ As you enter the queue for the Radiator Springs Racers, you will come to a rock formation with a water spring around it. According to the sign above, this is the _____ wonder of the world.

   a. 8th   c. 12th

   b. 9th   d. 8 ¾

39. ★ As you read the signs around you look at the billboard above the queue. You will find a list of what this water does for you. Finish this line, "Turns back the _____."

   a. Odometer   c. Wear and Tear

   b. Miles   d. Years

40. ★ On the same billboard mentioned above, you will find another list of what this water does for you. Finish this line, "Eliminates Squeaks and _____."

   a. Knocks   c. Squawks

   b. Pings   d. Rattles

41. ★ As you read the variety of cap options at Stanley's Cap and Tap, how much is the cap for Desoto?

   a. 15 cents   c. 20 cents

   b. 10 cents   d. 35 cents

42. ★ What is the price for the Maxwell cap at Stanley's?

   a. 25 cents   c. 125 cents

   b. 100 cents   d. 75 cents

43. ★★ As you enter the structure with the bottles in the walls, stop and read the sign describing the building. How far to the moon would these bottles stretch end to end?

   a. 126 times   c. 126 Millionths

   b. 126 thousandths   d. 126 miles

44. ★★ As you enter your ride vehicle and begin your journey, what is the company name of the truck you almost collide with?

   a. Dinoco
   c. Rusteze
   b. Lightning McQueen
   d. Mater's Junkyard

45. ★ As you race with the train and are stopped by the police, finish the warning you receive: "Whoa, slow down. You're not _____ yet."

   a. Racing
   c. Finished
   b. Driving
   d. Speeding

46. ★ As you find Mater he takes you tractor tipping. What did you do to make the tractors tip?

   a. Bump them
   c. Squeal your tires
   b. Roll them
   d. Honk your horn

47. ★★ As you enter Radiator Springs, what do you see fly across the moon?

   a. Mater
   c. Doc Hudson
   b. Lightning McQueen
   d. Luigi

48. ★★★ On race day you will enter either Ramon's or Luigi's business. As you enter Ramon's, how many paint samples do you see on display?

   a. 12
   c. 18
   b. 14
   d. 10

49. ★★★ Which color is seen in the center car in the top row of the paint samples at Ramon's?

   a. White
   c. Pink
   b. Blue
   d. Green

50. ★★ If you enter the Luigi's side to get ready for the race, what sort of tires does he give you for the race?

a. White walls   c. Off road

b. Green walls   d. Wheel walls

51. ★★ As you exit your makeover, you find Doc Hudson getting you ready to race. Which of these companies manufactures alternators according to the signs above?

a. Mood   c. Re-Volting

b. Retread   d. Vitoline

52. ★ Which of these colors is *not* seen in the wig Guido is wearing at the start of the race?

a. Red   c. White

b. Green   d. Blue

53. ★ At the end of your race, at what landmark do you find yourself?

a. Radiator Caverns   c. Stalactite Caverns

b. Tail Light Caverns   d. Materama Caverns

54. ★ As you approach Mater and Lightening McQueen, who does Lightening say won the race?

a. You did   c. No one did

b. They did   d. We all did

Looking for hints on your way? Click here to find what you seek.

Pacific Wharf

Pacific Wharf sends you to the foggy bay of San Francisco where you can sample classic Ghirardelli chocolates or Boudin sourdough bread. Stroll through the bay and enjoy a bowl of hot soup or yummy Chinese food, whatever your taste in this quaint area of Disney's California Adventure.

Boudin's Bakery Tour

1. ★★ As you enter the Boudin Sourdough factory, what is the patented name for the bacteria used in this bread?
    a. Lactobacillus San Francisco
    b. Lactobacillus Sourdough

c. Lactobacillus Golden Gate

d. Lactobacillus Boudin

2. ★ How many hours from start to finish does it take bakers to make a loaf of sourdough bread?

a. 72   c. 48

b. 24   d. 128

3. ★ As you enter the bread-making area, what is the name of the machine used to allow the bread to relax?

a. Overhead Relaxer   c. Overhead Proofer

b. Overhead Puffer   d. Overhead Ride

4. ★★ When the dough is in the refrigerator, which of these is *not* one of the changes it goes through?

a. Flavor   c. Color

b. Texture   d. Size

5. ★ As you exit the bakery tour and continue to wander through Pacific Wharf you will come across a photo opportunity in a net of fish. How many tons of fish are in the net?

a. 7 ½   c. ¼

b. 7 ¼   d. 197 ½

Did you know?
You can pop into Ghirardelli to pick up a sample of delicious chocolate or treat yourself to a sundae.

Looking for hints on your way? Click here to find what you seek.

Paradise Pier

Enter the days of boardwalk thrills in this sea side area of California Adventure. Try your hand at arcade games or get your thrills on the attractions along the shore. Finish your day at the sea shore with the thrills of World of Color.

The Little Mermaid Ariel's Undersea Adventure

1. ★★ As you enter the queue for The Little Mermaid Ariel's Undersea Adventure, you will notice a large mural behind the loading queue. How many flags do you see on Prince Eric's castle total?

   a. 5   c. 6
   b. 3   d. 15

2. ★ As you look at the mural, what does Prince Eric hold in his hand?

   a. Seashell   c. Trident

   b. Spyglass   d. Miniature Boat

3. ★ As your journey begins, you will find Scuttle the seagull narrating your story. What item does Scuttle have in his hands?

   a. Accordion   c. Spyglass

   b. Guitar   d. Storybook

4. ★★★ As you catch your first glimpse of Ariel above you, how many sea horses do you find watching her sing?

   a. 5   c. 10

   b. 9   d. 12

5. ★★★ As you listen to Ariel's song in her collection room, how many thing-a-ma-bobs does she have?

   a. 10   c. 50

   b. 30   d. 20

6. ★ As you watch Ariel in her collection room, what object does Sebastian the crab pop out of?

   a. Helmet   c. Jewelry Box

   b. Crown   d. Book

7. ★ As you enter the Under the Sea party, how many tentacles does the octopus have?

   a. 6   c. 8

   b. 7   d. 9

8. ★★ As you pass by the fish playing drums to your right, how many fish are in the conga line?

   a. 4   c. 6

   b. 5   d. 7

9. ★ What instrument does the green fish play at the end of the Under the Sea party?

   a. Clarinet   c. Drums

   b. Saxophone   d. Flute

10. ★★ As you enter Ursula's lair, listen to her song. Finish this line: "I'll admit that in the past I've been a _____."

   a. Nasty   c. Stinker

   b. Witch   d. Patsy

11. ★ As you rise out of the sea and onto land once again, what type of birds hold open the canopy for you to pass?

   a. Seagulls   c. Pelicans

   b. Doves   d. Cranes

12. ★ As you watch Ariel and Prince Eric in their row boat, what color ribbon is tied in Ariels hair?

   a. Pink   c. Purple

   b. Yellow   d. Blue

13. ★ What do the ducks use for instruments as they accompany Sebastian serenading Ariel and Prince Eric?

   a. Frogs   c. Turtles

   b. Fish   d. Crabs

14. ★ As you celebrate the marriage of Ariel and Prince Eric, how many lobsters do you see dancing with joy?

   a. 3   c. 7

   b. 4   d. 1

- -

Did you know?

As you exit the Little Mermaid ride look to your left and you will see a tiny cameo of Hans Christian Andersen, the writer of The Little Mermaid. Also, you will see a cameo of the *Little Mermaid* statue in Denmark.

- -

· · · · · · · · · · · · · · ·

15.　★★ As you move forward on your discovery of Paradise Pier, cross over the boardwalk opposite Ariel's Grotto. You will find some vintage billboards on your way. In the Coca Cola billboard, how many bottles of soda pop do you find?

a.　7　　　　　　　　　　c.　4

b.　8　　　　　　　　　　d.　6

16.　★★★ In the billboard for Paradise Pier, how many umbrellas do you find on the beach?

a.　15　　　　　　　　　c.　17

b.　16　　　　　　　　　d.　21

17.　★★★ As you stand on the pier, listen closely to the voice doing the countdown for California Screamin'. Which famous actor's voice do you hear?

a.　Kurt Russell

b.　Val Kilmer

c.　Michael J. Fox

d.　Neil Patrick Harris

Toy Story Midway Mania

Did you know?

As you enter the queue for Toy Story Midway Mania, you will pass a large Mr. Potato Head. You will hear Mr. Potato Head sing and interact with the crowd periodically. Ask him to pull off his ear and watch what happens.

------

18.   ★★ As you weave your way around the queue for Toy Story Midway Mania, take a look at the posters for the attractions you will experience. For the Dino Darts poster, who is featured on the poster with Rex?

    a.   Trixie   c.   Woody

    b.   Slinky   d.   Jessie

19.   ★★ On the Green Army Men Shoot Camp poster, finish this line, "Aim for the _____, soldiers!"

    a.   Plates   c.   Toys

    b.   Target   d.   Stars

20.   ★★ In the Hamm and Eggs toss poster, what point value is assigned to the ducks?

    a.   100   c.   1000

    b.   500   d.   2000

21.   ★★ As you enter the loading queue, read some of the signs around you. How many games of skill will you find?

    a.   4   c.   5

    b.   3   d.   7

22.   ★ As you read the signs around the loading queue what does the sign say about batteries?

    a.   Sold Separately   c.   Not Needed

    b.   Included   d.   Not Included

23.   ★ As you enter the ride vehicle and enter the game, what sea creature is featured on the playing card in front of you?

    a.   Seahorse   c.   Octopus

    b.   Crab   d.   Clam

24.   ★★ What sort of objects are you throwing during your practice game?

    a.   Balloons   c.   Pies

    b.   Darts   d.   Plates

25.   ★★ As you travel down the corridor with the board games piled up, which Disneyland inspired game do you find stacked on the right?

    a.   Fantasyland Game

    b.   Tomorrowland Game

    c.   Frontierland Game

    d.   Adventureland Game

26.   ★★★ As you quickly pass by the Candyland board game, what color tile must you select when you land on Cherry Pitfall?

    a.   Blue   c.   Green

    b.   Red   d.   Orange

27.   ★★★ Keep an eye out for the large wooden puzzle. Which piece is missing from the puzzle?

    a.   Ice Cream   c.   Carousel

    b.   Clown   d.   Cotton Candy

Did you know?

If you hit the mouse crawling up the side of the barn, you will trigger the barn to rotate 180 degrees. Hit the three mice within the barn and you will open several targets worth more points.

Did you know?

As you come to the Dino Darts game, aim for the long balloons at the top of the volcano. After you hit the three long balloons you will trigger the volcano to erupt balloons.

Did you know?

As you arrive at the army men plate break, hit the two plates that jump up with the 2000 point values. This will open the mountain and a tank will shoot plates at you worth 5000 points each.

28.   ★★★ As you leave the plate-breaking game, what circus animal is going to jump through the hoop on the puzzle?

    a.   Elephant   c.   Seal

    b.   Lion   d.   Giraffe

29.   ★★★ What is the name of the ice cream stand you see just before arriving at the Alien game?

    a.   Mickey Mouse   c.   Hockey Puck

    b.   Mr. Potato Head   d.   Animal Crackers

Did you know?

At the alien ring toss, hit all of the aliens in the center of the rocket ship. If you make them all disappear at one time, you will trigger a robot to open his mouth for you to shoot rings into for extra points.

Did you know?

When you arrive at Woody's Rootin' Tootin' Shootin' Gallery, hit each target to open them all up. Clear the board and targets worth 1000 and 2000 points will fill the board for you to hit.

Once you finish this part of the board, you will travel along. Hit the targets worth 1000 and 2000 points close to the bottom of the screen.

As the mine cars appear, hit the bat hanging above two times to make the mine cars worth 5000 points each. When the target appears in the finale, hit it as fast as you can to make the target worth more points.

30. ★ As you arrive at the points total screen, once you find out which animal level you hit, pull the string on your gun. What comes out on the screen?

a. Balloons   c. Suction cups
b. Darts   d. Confetti

31. ★ As you exit this attraction, you will come to a room at the top of the stairs. What stuffed animal is found under the desk?

a. Rabbit   c. Dog
b. Mouse   d. Bear

32. ★★ On the top of the desk you see there is a small brass plate. What do the words read on this plate?

a. Winners Only   c. Walt Disney
b. No Trespassing   d. No Admittance

33. ★ Across from Toy Story Midway Mania you will find a news stand. If you read the headline on the stack of newspapers, at what theater did Steamboat Willie premier?

a. Carthay Circle   c. Hyperion

b. Colony   d. Grauman's Chinese

34. ★ What is the price for *Modern Priscilla* magazine on the news stand?

a. 25 cents   c. 20 cents

b. 30 cents   d. 10 cents

35. ★ Which magazine is seen in the case lying sideways instead of right side up?

a. *Nature*   c. *Life*

b. *Harper's Bazaar*   d. *Harper's Weekly*

36. ★★ What page number are you told to look at according to the cover of *Science and Invention* magazine?

a. 829   c. 982

b. 892   d. 1002

37. ★★ Read the copy of the *Paradise Pier Post* on display at this news stand. If you read the articles along the Items of Interest, what is the disposition of the hogs found in Evansville Indiana?

a. Ferocious   c. Lazy

b. Gentle   d. Dangerous

Did you know?

As you stroll down the boardwalk, you can play old-fashioned arcade-style games and win prizes. Try your hand at Goofy About Finshin', Dumbo Bucket Brigade, or Casey at the Bat.

38. ★ As you approach Point Mugu Tattoo on the boardwalk, read the warning signs outside on the pillars. What do some hats contain?

a. Hair	c. Flowers
b. Heads	d. Rabbits

39.　★★ As you enter the store, you will see photo's of several tattooe'd persons. According to the small brass plate, which museum supplied the photos?

a. Smithsonian	c. Natural History
b. Circus World	d. MOMA

40.　★ As you enter the hat room, finish this sign: "Free Hats _____."

a. Tomorrow	c. Next Week
b. Today	d. Never

41.　★ As you find the large hats above your head, what color is the propeller on the baseball cap?

a. Red	c. Green
b. Blue	d. Yellow

42.　★ What color are the polka dots on the large blue hat with the brim above you?

a. Green	c. Pink
b. Purple	d. White

43.　★★ As you continue looking at the large hats above your head, which hat would be the only one worn for a job?

a. Police

b. Fireman

c. Baker

d. Construction Worker

44.　★ Read the signs above your head, which type of hat is on clearance?

a. Top hats	c. Pillbox
b. Sombrero's	d. Bowler

45. ★ As you enter the next section of the stores, you will find a mural of the fat lady on the wall. According to this mural, how much did she weigh?

a. 500 pounds   c. 6 ¾ ounces

b. 592 pounds   d. 529 pounds

46. ★ As you read the side show signs above the clothing displays, what act does Swalli Baba perform?

a. Sword Swallowing

b. Lying on Bed of Nails

c. Fire Eating

d. Rope Climbing

47. ★★ What is the name of the strongest man in the store as you read the side show signs?

a. Baron Big Pants   c. Tiny Tonnage

b. Sylvester the Strong   d. Melvin the Weak

48. ★ As you find the sign for Vipera's , finish the description on her sign: "Charming and _____."

a. Alluring   c. Startling

b. Irresistible   d. Alarming

49. ★ If you step outside the store and read the sign on the pillar, how many holes does each T-shirt include?

a. Four   c. Two extra

b. Six   d. Eight

50. ★ As you continue strolling around the lake, you will arrive at Silly Symphony Swings. You will find several posters for animated cartoons. How many seals appear on the *Mickey's Circus* poster?

a. 1   c. 4

b. 2   d. 3

51. ★★ On the poster for *Mickey's Opera*, Which character appears on the poster with Mickey Mouse?

    a. Goofy
    c. Daisy Duck
    b. Donald Duck
    d. Minnie Mouse

52. ★ In the poster for *The Whoopee Party*, what color are Minnie's shoes?

    a. Pink
    c. Green
    b. Red
    d. Black

53. ★★ In the poster for *The Band Concert*, how many musical notes do you find?

    a. 10
    c. 30
    b. 13
    d. 52

Did you know?

As you work your way around the back side of the lake, you will find hidden treasures like the food court, Jumpin' Jellyfish and the Goofy's Sky School attractions.

---

54. ★★ As you arrive at Seaside Souvenirs, take a look at the large sign above. How many seashells do you find in the bucket?

    a. 6
    c. 2
    b. 4
    d. 12

55. ★ Along the back wall of Seaside Souvenirs you will find a submarine. What famous submarine is depicted here?

    a. USS Triton
    c. Red October
    b. USS Disney
    d. The Nautilus

Looking for hints on your way? Click here to find what you seek.

As you finish your tour of the Disneyland resort, I hope you have seen the parks through new eyes. First time guests, my hope is to help you get the most out of your time. Frequent visitors, if you found even two new attractions to, I have succeeded in my mission.

My love of all things Disney continues daily knowing a new thrill is waiting for me next time I visit the parks. Never would I want to have a day when I did not find something new to fall in love with at Disneyland resort.

The Author

Catherine Olen

Answer Key

Disneyland

ESPLANADE

1. C-32
2. D-650 million
3. A-138 Feet
4. A-Yesterday

MAIN STREET U.S.A.

1. A-Mr. and Mrs. Darling
2. B-1955
3. D-W.E. Disney

Disneyland Fire Station

4. C-105
5. D-912
6. A-2:31

7. B-1894 - 1899
8. C-Greenberg
9. A-Jess and Bess

Main Street Train Station

10. D-1/8th
11. A-173
12. D-Bill Justice
13. C-004565
14. C-Big Thunder Mountain
15. B-Chicago
16. C-Broggie
17. D-Watling
18. C-1871
19. D-6

Disneyana

20. D-2:05
21. B - Mosler Safe

Main Street Opera House

22. C-Drinking fountain
23. B-Fond
24. A-Genie
25. C-1:100
26. A-50,000
27. D-$1.20
28. B-Donald Duck
29. B-1965
30. C-Cowboy
31. D-The Capitol Building
32. A-Unfinished work
33. D-1863
34. A-Walter Pfieffer
35. A-Lucille Ball
36. D-Determination
37. B-1948

Main Street Magic Shop

38. D-Steve Martin
39. B-David Copperfield

Emporium

40. C-98

41. D-Dentist

Main Street Cinema

42. B-Tilly
43. C-Fifi
44. A-Identification Check
45. B-1895
46. C-People
47. B-No moustache
48. A-Eye patch
49. D-Carolwood

Crystal Arcade

50. C-107
51. B-1855
52. C-Teeter Totter
53. D-Captain Hook

Penny Arcade

54. A-Esmeralda
55. B-Bull Montana
56. A-Dynamite
57. C-The Adventures of Charlie Chaplin
58. D-M. Welte & Sohne
59. B-We Never Sleep
60. B-Piano
61. A-Laughing Gas

Disney Clothiers

62. C-Peter Pan and Tinker Bell
63. D-Wooden solider
64. B-Purdue
65. D-Wizard of Bras
66. A-Walt Disney

HUB

1. C-A clown
2. C-Partners
3. B-Fantasy
4. D-Tinker Bell

FANTASYLAND

Sleeping Beauty Castle

1. A-"When you wish upon a star, your dreams come true"
2. C-July 17, 1995
3. C-2035
4. B-Disney family crest
5. D-Squirrels
6. B-Break
7. D-Sure
8. A-3
9. C-Spinning wheels
10. B-Green light
11. C-Blue
12. D-Till the princess awakes
13. D-Demons
14. A-Dragon
15. B-Maleficent
16. B-The End
17. D-Peter Pan
18. C-The Evil Queen

Snow White's Scary Adventure

19. D-Beware
20. A-Sleeping Death
21. B-Owl
22. D-Red and white
23. C-Grumpy
24. A-Evil Queen's castle
25. D-Vultures
26. B-Peacock
27. D-Green
28. B-Crocodiles
29. B-Dopey
30. A-5
31. C-Skull
32. C-Happy

Peter Pan's Flight

33. A-Big Ben
34. D-The rooftops

35. C-Peter Pan
36. B-Two stars
37. B-Rainbow
38. C-Tiger Lily
39. D-4
40. A-"Smee!"
41. C-3

Pinocchio's Daring Journey
42. B-Cow
43. C-Stromboli's Theater
44. D-Bags of gold
45. C-Cleo and Figaro
46. B-Dutch girl
47. C-Lock
48. D-Red
49. B-Popcorn
50. D-Ring the bell
51. A-The Rough House
52. D-Moonshine jugs
53. C-The Mona Lisa
54. B-To The Salt Mines
55. C-"Watch Out!"
56. A-Lying in bed
57. B-The Blue Fairy

King Arthur's Carousel
58. A-Rightwise
59. C-Orange

60. C-58

Mr. Toad's Wild Ride
61. B-6
62. D-Semper Absurda
63. A-Ratty's House
64. B-Toads
65. C-6
66. A-Sir Clinksalot
67. B-Boxing
68. D-Chicken leg
69. B-41
70. A-6
71. B-Beer mugs
72. C-"Guilty! Thank you, that is all"
73. D-Blue Boy

Casey Junior's Circus Train
74. C-Monkeys
75. A-"I Think I Can!"
76. B-6

Dumbo
77. A-Mouse
78. C-16
79. B-Alice
80. A-59
81. C-Cheshire Cat

82. A-Pink
83. B-9

Storybook Land Canal Boats
84. D-44
85. B-The Three Little Pigs
86. C-The Water Wheel
87. A-Peter Pan
88. C-A Whole New World
89. B-Mine car
90. D-Pumpkin
91. C-Pink
92. A-Desert plants
93. A-Lullaby Land
94. C-Tinker Bell
95. B-King Tritons Castle
96. D-The Three Mills

Mad Tea Party
97. D-Pink
98. A-4
99. B-18

Alice in Wonderland
100. B-Blue
101. D-Hammer
102. C-Cheshire Cat
103. B-White

104. A-"Looking for the White Rabbit?"
105. B-Yellow
106. C-Golden Afternoon
107. D -12
108. C-Weeds
109. B-Beyond
110. A-Accordion
111. A-"Rule 42, the queen always wins."
112. D-Spades
113. C-Pink
114. A-Abominable Snowman
115. B-May 27, 1978

It's a Small World
116. C-14
117. B-24
118. D-Blue
119. A-Koala
120. B-6
121. C-Eiffel Tower
122. C-Italy
123. A-Hearts
124. C-Aladdin and Jasmine
125. D-4
126. B-Mushu
127. A-Pink

128. C-8
129. B-Sombreros
130. B-Guitar
131. A-Aloha
132. D-Lilo and Stitch
133. A-Butterflies
134. D-Lasso
135. C-Weather's Nice

Snow White's Grotto
136. A-Hearts
137. B-"I'm Wishing"
138. C-Owls
139. C-Grumpy

Fantasy Faire
140. B-Rapunzel
141. D-10,000
142. A-Blue
143. B-Bird Watching
144. D-3
145. A-Sore

TOONTOWN
1. B-Mouse
2. C-A Smile
3. D-Sunshine
4. D-38
5. A-Ski Jump

6. C-Hockey puck

Goofy's Playhouse
7. B-Roger Rabbit
8. B-Crow
9. A-Carrots
10. D-7
11. C-Grape jelly
12. B-Underwear
13. C-Silly Scales in G
14. C-Milk bottle
15. D-Yellow

Donald Duck's Boat
16. A-Red
17. B-Miss Daisy
18. C-4
19. D-Rain hat
20. B-Starfish

Gadget's Go Coaster
21. A-Ruler
22. B-Acorns
23. D-Toothbrush
24. A-Rubber bands
25. C-Drinking straws
26. B-Dominos
27. C-55
28. D-Walnut

29. A-Thimble
30. C-Nickel
31. D – Chinny Chin Chin
32. B-Do not run with
33. C-Sardine can
34. A-Max Power
35. B-Peanut butter

Mickey Mouse House

36. A-Ace
37. D-Hockey stick
38. B -1400
39. C-Toontown Little League
40. D-The Big Cheesy
41. A-Call Minnie
42. C-Hick Rooster
43. B-24
44. A-Mouseway
45. D-Slipper
46. C-7
47. B-Mice Skating
48. A-Fabric Hardener
49. B-February 1942
50. D-Society Dog Show
51. C-Toontown Hotel
52. B-The Movie Barn
53. A-3

54. A-Croc's cloaks
55. B-31
56. D-Yup
57. C-Paper

Minnie Mouse House

58. A-60-70
59. C-Jessica's Secret
60. B-Red
61. A-Herman Mouse
62. D-He is very busy at the movie barn
63. C-Cheesemore
64. B-10 oz
65. C-Cheese Cake
66. A-They're diet
67. B-Baking soda
68. D-Cheese
69. C-Cheese
70. D-Wrong Turn
71. B-Jessica Rabbit
72. A-Sock
73. B-Honk
74. D-Air
75. C-Bruiser
76. C-Dry Water
77. D-3rd Little Piggy
78. A-Pig
79. B-Scrooge McDuck

80. C-1928
81. C-Laugh O' Gram Films
82. B-Gray
83. C-Mouse trap
84. A-One Liners
85. D-W. Giant
86. B-Paint
87. A-Guffaw
88. C-Meow
89. B-Chip and Dale
90. A-Gone Fishing
91. C-Falling down rabbit holes

Roger Rabbit's Cartoon Spin
92. D-IM L8
93. A-ZPD2DA
94. B-40
95. C-11:45
96. B-Ballet
97. D-5
98. C-Giants
99. A-Travel in Pairs
100. A-Fluorine
101. B-Television
102. C-8:05
103. D-2
104. B-Jessica

105. A-Spin
106. B-Wishing apples
107. C-Stand Clear
108. D-Straight jacket
109. A-E=MC2
110. C-Rubber wieners
111. B-4
112. A-J
113. D-Stars
114. B-Elephant
115. A-Mr. Tailpipe
116. C-Stapler

ADVENTURELAND
1. C-Wood
2. B-5
3. D-Eagle
4. A-Future
5. C-56
6. D-Freeze
7. A-Boats
8. B-Tortuga
9. D-Somewhere in the Congo
10. A-Mosquito nets
11. D-Gorilla

Enchanted Tiki Room
12. B-Koro

13. C-Volcanoes
14. D-16-Disneyana, City Hall, Carnation Café, Plaza Inn, Space Moutain Exit, The Enchanted Tiki Room, Adventureland Entrance, New Orleans Square, Hungry Bear Resturant, Village Haus Resturant, Fantasyland Theater, Toontown, Alice in Wonderland, Big Thunder Ranch, Pirates Lair (2), Rancho del Zocalo Restaurante'
15. A-Frederick
16. B-In the audience
17. C-Hair
18. D-Juanita
19. A-Rosita
20. B-Birds of Paradise
21. A-The Shower
22. C-The Gods
23. C-Heigh Ho

The Jungle Cruise
24. D-Water

25. C-1921
26. D-Cairo
27. B-Air Morocco
28. C-Nile
29. A-Pat
30. D-Ginger
31. A-17
32. B-They have their trunks on
33. A-Bertha
34. C-Lantern
35. B-Albert Falls
36. C-The Nile
37. C-3
38. D-Hyenas
39. B-Wiggling their ears
40. C-Skulls
41. D-Spears
42. D-The back side of water
43. A-Python
44. C-Shrunken Heads

Indiana Jones Adventure
45. B-Temple of the Forbidden Eye
46. D-Green
47. B-Rubble
48. D-Bats

49. C-Spikes
50. A-Diamond
51. B-Sallah
52. D-Slingshot
53. A-Take Heed
54. D-Eye on the Globe
55. B-Club Obi Wan
56. D-12
57. C-Wall moves
58. A-Mirrors
59. D-Brakes
60. B-Beauty
61. C-Beyond the gates of doom
62. A-Swerve left
63. D-3
64. C-Cobra
65. D-Snake! You're on your own
66. A-Spears
67. B-Gold pieces
68. C-Wisely
69. A-Distilled Water
70. D-Life

Tarzan's Treehouse
71. C-Mind Thy Head
72. A-Edgar Rice Burroughs

73. D-Lace
74. B-Kala
75. C-Tarzan as he grows up
76. D-Amber Lion
77. D-Blue
78. A-Fear
79. C-Quill
80. B-Blue
81. C-Mrs Potts and Chip
82. A-Superior
83. D-137

FRONTIERLAND
1. D-Revolutionary
2. B-1775
3. A-Fire step
4. B-Ft. Bragg
5. C-Antlers
6. D-1807

Westward Ho Trading Company
7. B-Heart
8. C-Molasses
9. D-Lard

Shooting Exposition
10. C-Frown
11. D-December 21

12. B-6
13. A-Saw
14. C-Short Change
15. A-3

Pioneer Mercantile
16. A-14
17. B-Woody's Roundup
18. C-Pocahontas and John Smith
19. D-American Wringer
20. C-10 Days
21. A-Bank robbers
22. D-Birmingham
23. C-Money bag
24. B-Canoe
25. A-Hides
26. C-90
27. A-Buffalo Bill Cody
28. A-Leather Jackets
29. D-Russel

Golden Horeshoe
30. A-Singers
31. B-Clean glasses
32. C-Ladies
33. D-14
34. D-Fish
35. A-13

36. C-Miss Taylor
37. B-Chicago
38. A-Whiskey
39. D-1845

The Mark Twain Riverboat
40. B-Columbia
41. B-Ghost stories
42. C-Brer Frog
43. D-Mark Twain
44. A-Peace
45. B-Plains
46. C-Shaman
47. D-Beaver
48. C-Pirate
49. A-Red River Valley

Big Thunder Mountain Railroad
50. C-2015
51. D-1880
52. C-Jumbo
53. A-1869
54. B-Best food in town
55. C-$100
56. B-10 cents
57. D-Jeremiah Colt
58. A-Wilderness
59. B-Dynamite
60. D-Mickey Mouse

TOMORROWLAND

1. D-Constructive
2. A-12

Buzz Lightyear Astro Blasters

3. C-Bad, Very Bad
4. B-112164
5. D-3
6. C-Gamma
7. A-Etch A Sketch
8. D-20464
9. B-Purple
10. A-Jacks
11. B-5
12. C-Zurg Rules
13. B-5
14. A-Pointless
15. D-Blue
16. A-$8.99
17. C-2070 7776
18. B-Space Scout
19. A-Galactic Hero
20. D-Golden Claw
21. C-Crab
22. B-Employee of the Millenium
23. D-Galactic Hero

Star Tours

24. A-Admiral Ackbar
25. C-Dust Contamination
26. B-IC360
27. C-Gate Changed
28. D-Landed
29. A-Hoth
30. D-Partly Cloudy
31. B-5
32. C-Droids
33. B-Pack in Styrofoam
34. C-Garrison
35. A-9

Autopia

36. B-Tankful
37. C-55
38. A-Mouse Crossing

Finding Nemo Submarine Voyage

39. D-10
40. A-Darla
41. B-Volcano
42. D-1 Year
43. C-To the EAC
44. D-Shell
45. A-Fabio
46. B-Balloons to Pop

47.   C-Jelly fish
48.   B-Chanting
49.   C-Ink
50.   A-Shell
51.   D-Blown out whale blowhole
52.   B-Mermaids
53.   B-3

NEW ORLEANS SQUARE

Pirates of the Caribbean

1.   C-30th
2.   B-March 7, 1997
3.   C-Tell No Tales
4.   D-Captain Blackbeard
5.   A-Oh! Susanna
6.   A-Avast There
7.   B-In every cove
8.   C-3
9.   D-Seagull
10.   D-Chess
11.   B-Parrot
12.   C-Harpsichord
13.   A-The Wicked Wench
14.   B-Carlos
15.   A-Bilge Rats
16.   B-Six bottles of rum
17.   C-6
18.   D-3
19.   B-Black and white
20.   B-A dog biscuit
21.   C-Piracy
22.   A-Isla Tesoro
23.   C-Fortune Red
24.   B-Rest Stop
25.   D-Paint
26.   C-4
27.   A-John Lafitte
28.   D-January 8, 1815
29.   B-1764

The Haunted Mansion

30.   D-Ghost Relations
31.   A-5
32.   C-August 9, 1869
33.   C-Rosie
34.   B-Seymour Butts
35.   D-7 Pet Cemetery front of Haunted Mansion, Pet Cemetery Rear of Haunted Mansion, Cemetery within Mansion, Fort Wilderness Cemetery, Exposition Shooting Gallery, Storybook Land Canal Alice in

Wonderland scene, Taj
Mahal in It's a Small
World

36. D-Ghoulish delight
37. A-Danger
38. B-George
39. C-A bone
40. B-Medusa
41. D-Donald Duck
42. A-Candlesticks
43. C-Ringing a bell
44. B-13
45. C-5
46. A-5
47. C-1877
48. D-George
49. D-Guitar
50. B-3
51. A-6
52. B-5
53. D-Ball and chain
54. B-Death certificate
55. C-Jonathon Winship
56. A-8

CRITTER COUNTRY

1. D-Turtle
2. B-Davy Crockett
3. B-Gomer

4. D-Hamburger
5. A-Carrots
6. B-Brer Rabbit

**The Many Adventures of
Winnie the Pooh**

7. C-Blue
8. D-Gopher
9. B-Chair
10. A-Winnie the Pooh
11. C-Under a window
12. B-Blue and green
13. D-What a wonderful
dream
14. C-Pooh's Birthday
15. A-8
16. D-Honey Remedies
17. B-4
18. A-Rabbit

Splash Mountain

19. D-Molasses Vats
20. C-7
21. B-Yesterday
22. A-Axe
23. B-My time
24. C-50 Feet
25. A-Chattanooga
26. D-14

27. D-Brer Skunk
28. C-Watermelon
29. B-Pumpkins
30. C-Frog
31. D-Turtle
32. A-Handcart
33. A-Frowns
34. B-Honey
35. C-4
36. C-Vultures
37. B-Doo Dah Landing
38. D-Organ
39. A-Andy
40. C-Bluebird
41. A-Extra Lens Caps
42. B-Picture Perfect
    Developer
43. D-Mr. Bluebird
44. D-Pooh's Birthday
45. C-Pooh's Hunny Mixer
46. A-1889
47. A-Rabbit's Garden
48. C-6
49. B-17
50. D-Goffer's

Disney's California Adventure

BUENA VISTA STREET

Oswald's Tires

1. A-Packard
2. C-1935
3. B-December 1, 1922
4. A-U
5. D-30
6. A-7
7. C-February 8, 2001
8. B-Dreamers

Mortimers Market

9. B-California Limited
10. D-Wednesday
11. A-Salmon
12. C-Radio
13. C-Big Top Toys
14. B-701
15. C-80

Julius Katz & Sons

16. A-Newfangled Television
17. A-Ugly
18. B-Blue? Really?
19. C-I'm a Little Teapot

20. D-5
21. B-Disney
22. D-1

Trolley Treats

23. C-Candy Mountain
24. A-Chocolate Kisses
25. C-5 Cents
26. D-Jelly Beans
27. B – Fish

Five and Dime

28. B-25 Cents
29. D-3

Big Top Toys

30. C-3
31. D-Green
32. A-Storytellers
33. B-Cardboard
34. D-111828
35. C-Pen

Carthay Circle

36. A-Valet
37. C-Lillian Disney
38. B-Shirley Temple

GRIZZLY PEAK AIRFIELD

1. B-Aircraft
2. C-Canoe
3. D-Red

Humphrey's

4. B-Nature's Half Acre
5. A-Humphrey's
6. C-Star Gazers
7. B-725-740
8. C-Bird Watching
9. A-No Man's Bluff
10. D-26 cents

Smokejumpers Grill

11. C-The Parent Trap
12. B-1957
13. C-Mud
14. D-Ranger Headquarters
15. A-Little Growlers Club
16. A-Grilled Chicken
17. B-Accordion
18. C-Joy Riding
19. A-Hotshots
20. D-Cream
21. C-Mt. Muir
22. B-John Muir
23. B-Conservation Pledge

Soarin' Over California

24. A-Patrick Warburton
25. C-Mickey ears
26. D-Little Aviators
27. A-San Francisco
28. C-9
29. B-Hang glider
30. B-6
31. A-Christmas

GRIZZLY PEAK

Grizzly River Run

1. D-Lantern
2. A-8
3. A-A saw
4. C-Fish Frozen
5. B-Toboggan
6. C-4
7. A-Eagle
8. D-10,457
9. C-Mining pan
10. A-Dirt Demon
11. B-Pedal to the Metal
12. A-Cold Shower
13. C-Eureka

Redwood Creek Challenge Trail

14. D-Squirrel Scramble

15. B-Kevin
16. C-The Moon
17. C-Clarinet
18. A-Leaving footprints
19. B-To watch his family
20. D-Axe
21. C-Never mind – Bear
    Got it
22. B-Kilo
23. C-1 Year
24. A-818
25. D-Volcanic eruption
26. B-1848
27. D-15 Feet
28. C-Cows drinking
29. A-Rocks
30. B-Canoe storage
31. D-Snowmobiles

HOLLYWOOD

1. D-Menswear
2. A-Supporting
3. C-Underwood
4. B-Walt Disney
   Productions
5. A-Pinocchio
6. A-Violation

Off the Page

7. B-Minnie Mouse
8. C-79
9. D-Dopey
10. A-Tick Tock Croc
11. C-Green
12. C-Pain and Panic
13. B-Blue
14. B-Sewing the dress
15. A-Pulling Ariel's tail
16. D-Mulan
17. C-Zazu

Schmoozie's

18. A-Blue
19. B-Pink
20. C-Dinosaur
21. D-14
22. C-Train
23. B-Grocer
24. A-Blue
25. A-9735
26. D-Berlin
27. A-$453
28. C-5
29. B-Crest

Monster's Inc., Mike and Sulley to the Rescue

30. A-Screamy
31. B-10:27
32. C-Fire Blechers
33. D-6
34. C-7
35. A-Cyclops
36. B-Latte
37. C-Vulture
38. D-Cold Saki
39. A-Glob
40. C-Bag O Calories
41. D-Same Old
42. B-5
43. B-Super Natural
44. A-916
45. D-00002
46. A-Happy Birthday
47. B-Mangle Fruit
48. C-He was rolled up and down like a yoyo
49. C-Uh oh
50. B-Yellow
51. D-2319
52. C-2:00
53. D-Comb
54. B-47
55. A-Terrifying
56. B-1

Twilight Zone Tower of Terror

57. A-1929
58. D-Cribbage
59. C-403
60. B-Shirley Temple
61. C-The Wizard of Oz
62. A-Hysterics
63. D-Drowned in lake
64. B-Needlepoint
65. D-Screen Guide
66. C-Room Service
67. A-Handkerchief
68. B-Los Angeles Examiner
69. A-1215
70. C-Tip Top Club
71. D-Billiards
72. A-Mahj ong
73. B-31
74. D-The Thing About Machines
75. A-8
76. C-Where is Everybody?
77. A-Costume Ball
78. D-Adam Grant
79. B-13

80. B-Danger Man in Boiler
81. A-3 Tons
82. C-The real world

A BUG'S LAND
1. A-Bug Sized
2. C-Drinking straw

It's Tough to be a Bug
3. A-10 Times
4. D-Hi mom
5. D-800,000
6. B-Beetles
7. C-Smell
8. B-Picky
9. A-Black Widow
10. C-15
11. B-40 Feet
12. D-5 Million
13. A-26,000
14. C-One Teaspoon
15. A-Jumping
16. B-300 million years
17. C-Chili
18. D-Acorns
19. B-I'll be back
20. A-Churros
21. C-Pill Bugs
22. B-Bug Doom
23. A-Rotten cupcake
24. D-Grasshoppers
25. C-Cowboy Crunchies
26. D-7
27. B-Tissue box
28. A-Sneezy
29. B-Milk carton
30. C-22
31. C-Homespun Applesauce
32. B-Sewing needle
33. D-45
34. D-6
35. A-Cotton swab
36. D-Purple
37. C-Popsicle sticks
38. B-28
39. C-Something to eat
40. A-Candy Corn
41. C-Become a beautiful butterfly
42. D-18
43. B-Gooey
44. A-Pencils

CARSLAND
1. B-Flo's
2. C-160

3.   A-Cogs

Taste In

4.   D-Free Range Seaweed

5.   B-Steroid Free

Mater's Junkyard Jamboree

6.   A-Rubberneck

7.   D-We can teach anyone to fly

8.   C-Impala XIII

9.   B-Private Eye

10.   B-Greater

11.   D-Tuesday

Cozy Cone Motel

12.   C-Cone on the Cob

13.   A-Stonehenge

14.   C-Buzz

15.   B-30

16.   A-Radios

Radiator Springs Curios

17.   D-Oil Slick

18.   A-Illinois

19.   C-Piston

20.   C-W857142

Flo's V8 Café

21.   B-63 Cents

22.   D-Freon

23.   C-Axle Grease

24.   A-4

25.   C-Many moons ago

26.   A-Ramon

27.   B-LOWGEARS

28.   D-Fuel Line Inlet

29.   B-6

30.   C-1960

31.   D-Confusion

32.   A-We Never Muffle the Truth

33.   A-Torque Wrench

34.   B-94 years

35.   D-27

36.   C-Drivers License

37.   B-Stanley

38.   D-8 ¾

39.   A-Odometer

40.   D-Rattles

41.   C-20 cents

42.   B-100 cents

43.   B-126 thousandths

44.   C-Rusteze

45.   A-Racing

46.   D-Honk your Horn

47.   A-Mater

48. B-14
49. C-Pink
50. A-White walls
51. C-Re-Volting
52. D-Blue
53. B-Tail Light Caverns
54. D-We all did

PACIFIC WHARF

Boudin's Bakery
1. A-Lactobacillus San Fransisco
2. A-72 Hours
3. C-Overhead Proofer
4. D-Size
5. B-7 ¼

PARADISE PIER

The Little Mermaid – Ariel's Adventure
1. C-6
2. B-Spyglass
3. A-Accordion
4. B-9
5. D-20
6. A-Helmet
7. C-8

8. C-6
9. B-Saxophone
10. A-Nasty
11. D-Cranes
12. D-Blue
13. C-Turtles
14. A-3
15. B-8
16. C-17
17. D-Neil Patrick Harris

Toy Story Midway Mania
18. A-Trixie
19. D-Stars
20. B-500
21. C-5
22. B-Included
23. A-Seahorse
24. C-Pies
25. D-Adventureland Game
26. D-Orange
27. A-Ice Cream
28. B-Lion
29. C-Hockey Puck
30. D-Confetti
31. C-Dog
32. A-Winners Only
33. B-Colony

34. C-20 cents
35. D-Harper's Weekly
36. C-982
37. A-Ferocious
38. D-Rabbits
39. B-Circus World
40. A-Tomorrow
41. D-Yellow
42. C-Pink
43. A-Police
44. B-Sombrero's
45. B-592 Pounds
46. A-Sword Swallowing
47. C-Tiny Tonnage
48. D-Alarming
49. A-Four
50. D-3
51. B-Donald Duck
52. C-Green
53. B-13
54. A-6
55. D-The Nautilus

Printed in the USA
CPSIA information can be obtained
at www.ICGtesting.com
JSHW022220140824
68134JS00018B/1177

9 781630 477769